Life—

ALWAYS A CHOICE OF DOORS

To Sheryl,

Life is as good —
live it and enjoy

Buck Lampe

10-3-14

Life—
ALWAYS A CHOICE OF DOORS

A Memoir by Ruth Lampe

Printed in the United States of America.

Publication Date: 04/05/2013

Library of Congress Control Number: 2013906116
ISBN 13:   Softcover   978-1-61856-238-8
                        Pdf   978-1-61856-239-5
                        ePub   978-1-61856-240-1
                        Kindle   978-1-61856-241-8

To order additional copies of this book, contact:
BookWhirl.com Publishing
PO Box 9031, Green Bay
WI 54308-9031, USA
www.BookWhirl.com

Contents

This memoir is dedicated to all my family.

"You will show me the path of life; in your presence is fullness of joy . . ."

(Psalm 16:11 NLT)

"Keep walking with me" may seem difficult but not when you look at it as a challenge and make your choice, one that would bring another path, another door.

I want you, the reader, to feel the love in our family and see my mother as she dealt with things in life that gave us all strength in the life we were to lead. It shows the love for a father that had a weakness for drinking but so many strengths to be a good and loving husband and father, and we loved that about him. It was respect and loving that I found in our family regardless of the problem we learned to overcome, and I have carried that on through my own life. Having parents giving you examples of how to deal with things in life gives you the tools to handle things because you remember this, and it brings it all full circle, family to family.

I wanted to tell about things that shaped my life. It has been a lot of doors, but the Lord helped me to have a discernment for the right things to follow, and I am grateful. It gave me the strength for the journey I would be taking with my sweet and gentle husband (as told in my first book, *Surviving Mental Illness*).

I am grateful for every day of my life because I have always known my direction, and it was always toward the Lord, my God. Life never comes to you in a package of no problems. I have learned to follow this "path of life," and it has been a joy even in the midst of all else.

Ruth Lampe, daughter, author

PREFACE

On the following pages, you will have impressive accounts of what went on in Toledo before and during the Great Depression. It is called *Tough Times in Toledo: The WPA Rebuilds a City, 1935 to 1941* by Michael Stockmaster.

Michael's research and knowledge will help all of us to understand and remember those days that grew so dim for us.

These were tough times. We, who lived it, have details in our hearts because we were a part of it. I lived it, my family lived it. Did this prepare us for what was yet to come? I believe it did. During the Great Depression we were separately suffering. Then came war preparation and the war and we pulled together and were one nation again, united.

And then, the memories of the long and painful time during WWII. Here again we are grateful to historians that gather these facts for us as proof that we were involved, we suffered, and we won the battle.

These records are kept for us to always remember those hard years of seeing the devastation that man is capable of.

The thing is, man can—and some do—turn things around. The one who only sees good in things and we rejoice in that. I am thinking of God's promise of if He could find one good man.

In this instance, He saw what a terrible place the world had become. He saw that no one cared about doing what was good and right anymore. And God saw their hearts. But... God also saw one good man. Would that ever be you or me?

These are the facts and they belong to all of us. (Genesis 6:9-7:10 God saw **one good man**. His name was Noah. Noah still cared about God. He listened to God, and he always tried to do what God said.)

Ruth Lampe 2013

WHAT DO WE SEE?
The grandeur of our life or the frustrations?

As you read these thoughts and poems, you will see the quiet influence of my mother, the concerns we had with my father, and the belonging we felt as a family. You may be wondering what brings me to this point in my writing this second book of mine, *Life—Always a Choice of Doors.*

If you have read my first book, *Surviving Mental Illness* (revised publication, May, 2013), you might see that I had to write this book relating now to my own early life because it prepared me in many ways to marry my dear husband, Rol, and to finish my road and our journey in strength and love, despite the pain at times and suffering. But "through it all," we had our love and each other.

Life, all along, is preparation for what is to come. Without it, we would not be able to live life that had love and quality and endurance to keep us on the path.

It all comes down to faith. "Faith is being . . . certain of what we do not see" (Hebrews 11:1)—genuine faith and allowing God to work in all circumstances. "Commit your way to the Lord; trust in Him, and He will do this." We can never realize His complete love for us until we commit. Faith isn't real until we walk through the hard situations in life and rely on

Him and commit to Him without hesitation. That is faith—that is when we feel His presence.

Ruth Lampe, Author

"If all were easy, and all were bright, where would the cross be? Where would the fight? But in the hard place, God gives to you, chances for proving what He can do." (Author, my mother, I believe)

> "You have made known to me the path of life; You will fill me
> with joy in your presence . . ."
>
> Psalm 16:11

One of my earliest and sweetest remembrances in growing up was when my father was in charge of putting us to bed because Mother went to an evening church service with neighbors.

This was a happy home. I felt it. Good grounding to starting a life of going through doors, the right door.

Mother said goodbye to each of us and reminded us that Daddy would be in charge. Oh, that caught my little girl's mind by surprise. Mother never left us, except maybe two times a year to go downtown Toledo. However, that evening I was having none of that. I started crying and I climbed on my Daddy's lap and cried and cried. Sorry Dad! The next morning I told Mom that I 'cry-ed on Daddy's shoit'. I can still see the sweet smelling white shirt I got all wet. The memory is so clear in my mind.

Our Mom always saw to it that Aunt Emma or someone special would be with us that long day and was a treat because she was so loving. It is not easy being comfortably away and leaving four young children.

For some years, Mom left early in the morning and walked to the end of the street to catch the bus to go downtown Toledo to do her shopping. Not only was she shopping, but she always did compartive shopping so she visited many stores before she made her final decision. The stores were located all over the downtown so it was quite a walk. At the end of the long day she would get back on the bus with her purchases travel to the bus stop where she had gotten on that morning, got off and then walked back down to our home. What a joy when she walked into the house with packages. Many things of necessity and then there was always something for us. I wonder now how could she carry all those things and not have a car to go back to, put them in and be relieved of the load she was caring. No wonder she only went every six months. Her life was her home my dad—and us and she did it well. She was a wonderful daughter and sister to her own family and she was a wonderful neighbor always. Those things represent the woman she was in so many ways.

'That, my first home, was the beginning of all the love I could wish for in my small world. A mother, a father, two brothers, and an older sister. I was the baby of the family, and I always liked that. Quite a distinction.

This was the beginning also of my own personal walk with the Lord, Jesus Christ. He was important to my family, and He became important to me. I felt a part of this relationship so much, and it strongly led me and continues to lead me. It was not hard to stay on the path. It was my desire.

At that time, we attended a small church in the area, and I so remember going to the pastor's home with other Sunday school kids and having a Christmas party. That was a wonderful fun, and I remember how bashful and quiet I was because I was new at parties with other people, and this was special. They gave out these little Christmas boxes of hard candy.

I remember so much about that sweet home with a wonderful green boulevard in the center of the street where all the parents racked leaves in the fall, and we jumped in them when the pile was big, and no one said "stop." It was family fun.

When Dad came driving in at dinnertime, he honked first before he approached the drive into the garage, and that was the sound my brothers were waiting for because they were ready to jump on the running board of the car and ride as far as the garage, holding on tightly.

And there were fields all around and so many play areas for the bigger kids. And there was an unused railroad track in the back, and I was allowed to go with the bigger kids, and on a summer's day, we would sit on the tracks in the morning sunshine and rub sandstone together and make it so smooth.

Perhaps it was because I didn't get to participate in all the fun the others did because I was so much younger; I began my life as an "observer of life" and have never stopped. That is something I love. I had a high school English teacher that wrote on a story I turned in, "Always keep a pencil with you and write down your observations." She saw that in me.

And we had walks with Mom on a summer eve.

We took these beautiful walks along the Maumee River almost every evening in the summer when we were little, and then on the way home, we ran around the mulberry tree—such peaceful memories. George, Bob, and I were within three and a half years of one another in age and Marie, six years older than me.

This was when we still lived on Glynn Court.

We had to move soon after that year in kindergarten. The Great Depression was such a difficult time for so many, but I never heard my parents argue or Mother cry because of what was happening to our life. They knew this new path had to be taken.

That door was walked through with my parents holding my hand.

This is a tribute I wrote in memory of my mother.

Walking Beside the Lord

This is my mom.

I truly believe it was my mother's dear hand in mine that made me see and feel Jesus' presence every day we had together since my birth.

How could it be other? The feeling of peace and joy it brought.

My mother's quiet joy in living brought joy to us all. Not that she always had it easy, but she made her life easy by remembering who loved her enough to protect her life and lead her to safety.

That is the way I have always felt. Safe. Because I knew who protected me and knew that special love He had to give me, same as my mother's love. It was like she was saying, "Thank You, Lord, for every minute of my life." I knew she could never thank our Lord enough. Never.

This is what came to me day after day with such force that I could not look away. She *knew* the Lord, and He knew her.

I can look back and see where my strength of character began, where my strength came from, and small decisions were made even then.

"His way is in the whirlwind and the storm."

Nahum 1:3

The next door my family had to walk through was not an easy path for a few years. We were in the hardest part of the Great Depression that was hitting our family hard. The year was about 1935. From my records, I gleaned that we were able to stay in our home on Glynn Court for almost five years from the beginning of the Great Depression. I know my father was in a large building construction, had his own business, and had a combination of buildings that were going up. The owners of the buildings could not pay because of their own financial difficulties, and the bank was only giving a small portion of your money to you, and that was what you had to live on. I was told by my brother George that Dad also bought out his two partners at that time.

My brother George found some evidence that Dad was a Canal Boulevard Supervisor from a Program from a dinner Dad attended with other supervisors. He was the opening speaker and talked on 'Grouping and Clustering of Men'. This was held on Saturday, March 24, 1934 in the Blue Room, Poole Hostelry, Maumee, Ohio - so here is evidence of how they were able to stay in the Glynn Court home after the Depression started until, possibly, the work finished. An article states "Toledo's Canals" The Anthony Wayne Trail, constructed in the 1930's, was built over much of the shared route of two canal systems— The Wabash and Erie, which joined Toledo with Indiana. These developments were responsible for the creation of the Great Lakes port city of Toledo.

It was not an easy time in Ohio or in our nation during those years of 1929 to 1939.

> "The strength of a ship is only fully demonstrated when it faces a hurricane, and the power of the gospel can only be fully exhibited when a Christian is subjected to some fiery trial. We must understand that for God to give 'songs in the night,' He must first make it night."
>
> Nathaniel William Taylor

This next part of the journey called life was difficult. Difficult because my dad's drinking—which I never witnessed before that I was aware of—took on depths and shadows in this picture of our life. I think of a piece of needlework and see how muddled it is on the back side, and it seems like a complete mess, but you turn it over, and you have a beautiful picture with its light colors and its shadows. The shadows represent the dark periods of life, but the picture would not be complete or have depth without these shadows. We were in the dark part, and it broke my heart, and it was always the heart of the rest of the family. We only lived in this rented home about eight months, I believe.

The Inevitable Door

So we left this wonderful neighborhood where I spent my first five years and walked into a gripping situation for the whole family because my father must have lost faith in being able to provide for his family, and he found his temporary peace with the bottle. Mother never allowed alcohol in the house. It was never mentioned, so I think that was an understood agreement. I was so young but old enough to see daily our pain and struggle.

Mom was a real protector, and we survived somehow. There are pictures in my mind that will always be there in my memory.

Our home life was desperate with his seemingly uncontrolled drinking, and Mom must have told Dad if he didn't stop, she would have to take us and leave until he straightened out. Mom just could not let us stay.

How could I forget that night? We were already in bed when Mom got us up, and we dressed, and we started walking away from the house, and my dad, standing on the sidewalk outside our house, seemed to sober up enough to say, "Bert, come back." Do you know what that does to little kids when they love their father so much? I can't begin to tell you what pain that brought. We were walking down the street, and Mom never turned around, but I did; we all must have. I think one of us said, "Mom, Dad needs us." Mom knew he would not straighten out his drinking until she took a stand. We heard Dad's sad voice, and it still resonates with me.

This then became our hardest period. Dad was unemployed, no work. (This was just before President Roosevelt took the brave step of starting many work programs, including the WPA—Work Projects Administration— where my dad finally found steady employment).

Soon after we departed that unhappy home, Dad was employed by the WPA, and that was our security until things changed about 1938 to 1939 with the bleak look of wars on the horizon and with the coming preparation of WWII.

Mom's decision proved to be right, and Dad, loving his family so much, improved quite a bit.

Unfortunately, Dad still kept the corner "beer joints" in business, and our life became one of anxiousness.

These were years when we struggled like the rest of the nation and the world because it affected not just us. It affected so many others.

We walked, probably ten blocks to my grandpa's home, and we stayed there eight months. A very hard eight months. So many adjustments. Grandpa didn't like children crying, and how do you ask a five-and-a-half-year-old to keep from crying? Everything stayed inside of me. I didn't have anyone to play with because it was an older neighborhood, and Mother didn't think I should walk back toward school to a friend's home. My brothers had each other, and my sister had friends. Other things happened also that were so hard for me. But on Sunday, and since we did not have a car, Dad got off the bus way down the street, and I stood in the middle of the street on a Sunday afternoon and searched and waited till I saw him walking toward me. Oh, Dad, that was the most wonderful sight. You have always been my hero.

Everything in life broke down until President Roosevelt saved us by implementing the work projects. It gave Dad his self-esteem back, and families regenerated. You could feel every step of the way.

If you have ever visited our national parks, you would see where craftsmen in the arts were also employed to create beautiful carved ceilings in the large lodges that were there. They stand today as a monument of survival.

We had to quietly adjust to other things also. At Grandpa's house, there were only three bedrooms—my grandpa's, my aunt's, which my mother shared, and then a small bedroom with a bed and a daybed.

Every week, we switched as to who slept in what combination. When you got the daybed, it was simply wonderful. However, in the other bed, my brothers slept at one end, and I at another, and I had two sets of feet in my face all night and didn't sleep good. (And I wasn't allowed to cry!) Mom sympathized with us, but she could not change things. We were to be grateful for this, and we were. Mom took care of the house while we stayed there and cooked and cleaned, and we were together as a unit, and that was good. We were thrilled and were taught to appreciate it. My mother showed such strengths during this time, and we felt it.

It was during this time that I came down with Scarletina and guess who got the bedroom all to herself. It was boring having no visitors, but then again, you had to figure I got the whole bedroom to myself. I don't have a clue where George, Bob, or Marie slept.

Eight months later, Dad and Mom told us they would be moving all of us into this rental home they found . . . my brother George told me that it was a new house, and the rent was $50, and we all would be together again. It was pure joy. We stayed in that home about five years and then were able to buy a home again and moved and had more stability. Three cheers for stability! Wherever we moved, my mother made it a home. She kept us clean, our home clean and was such a wonderful cook and baker. When things are intact, life goes on in a family, and it is wonderful because you are seemingly protected from outside forces. The Great Depression was an outside force, and it took its toll on us, temporarily. It wasn't that my dad stopped drinking, but he didn't drink out of pain anymore. His job with the WPA was supervising the building of swimming pools and parks so children and parents could have enjoyment even through hard times. He went to a lot of small towns surrounding Toledo and was gone from Sunday evening till Friday evening. This was a building time, a growth time for our family, and we had peace and calm all week, and no one coming home drunk, and life took on special times without a lot of uncertainties. These were the days of the radio and how it helped all of us. Such wonderful stories to listen to and comics that had radio shows we enjoyed in the living room. And reading became such a thing of joy to escape into a place in your mind that was so full of escape. When I was able to, I walked to the library on Saturdays to get some good books to read and enjoy.

Because of all Mom and Dad had gone through on losing their money, they were savers and very cautious. My mother and father saved three out of the four checks a month, and we lived on the one check. My dad was a supervisor on the job, so I think he did pretty well.

When Mom and Dad had saved a bit, the first thing Dad wanted to do is take us on a trip to Niagara Falls, and what a special time that was. I will always remember our time together. I was seven. We drove in our car; all of us crushed in together, and it must have taken a while because the highways are not fast or that good. I especially remember the darling little cabins we stayed in—Dad got two of them for our family—and what fun it was for us to run around that large area. It was not until I was going through some things of my mother's some years after she died, and I was at that time doing more memory writing, that I came across a picture of the cabins we stayed in. I was not sure how old I was at the time, and bless my mom, she had written on the back of the picture postcard "1937," and that made me seven. We were doing better, and I loved that my parents, with the first money they saved, cared so much about the family that they wanted to do this. I will always remember that trip and seeing those magnificent falls in their entire splendor. When I think of our family those years of 1935 to 1939, I remember them as "stand still" years when each family was trying to recoup gradually. But that family trip was a beautiful expression of love.

So we then had the busyness of having a nation prepare for the possibility of being involved in a war they did not want. Japan dropped their bombs on Pearl Harbor on December 7, 1941, and everything changed again.

War was declared, and our nation was fast preparing for the entry into this war, World War II. You know the story; we won but not without a lot of sacrifices. War was a busy time, and moms and dads worked long hours to help the war effort. Home life took on a different look, but there was love and continuity even in this. Our nation shifted from suffering personally to joining a suffering world.

I was given permission to include the following from the resource "Ohio History Central World War II."

"World War II formally began in September 1939, with Germany's invasion of Poland. Why another world war when WWI was a 'war to end all wars.' There are numerous reasons for why World War II began. Among the more important ones ranks a desire for Germany to reclaim land seized from it following the German defeat in World War I."

What helped bring America out of the Great Depression, which involved the whole World, was the urgency of helping in the war effort that started for us about 1939 as things got tense in the world and England so wanted our country to join them in the fight against Germany. It was getting closer and closer to becoming our war in America also; the continual news reports on the radio that kept us informed of the devastation of the war in Europe; the invasion of Japan on Pearl Harbor as it attacked on Sunday, December 7, 1941; the president of our nation declaring war on Germany and Japan right after Pearl Harbor. We were in the war for the duration. Peace accords were signed.

This then began World War II that took so many lives as we fought on two fronts. War, we always found out, brings jobs, and our nation once again had more work and could hire all those people who had been without work for so long. We saw it in Toledo, where I grew up.

"Every state found they had something to offer to our nation in helping with the war effort. 'Ohioans played a critical role in helping the United States attain victory in World War II. Approximately 839,000 Ohioans, roughly twelve percent of the state's entire population in 1940, served in the armed forces during the conflict. Of these men and women, twenty-three thousand of them died or were missing in action by the end of the war. Ohio civilians also actively participated in the war effort, joining scrap drives and growing victory gardens'—and my dad rented a portion of land from a farmer, and we had our victory garden."

"Tens of thousands of people also flocked to Ohio, seeking jobs in defense industries. Many of these workers came from Appalachia. Women also found ample opportunities for employment in defense plants and in the armed services. Companies like Willys-Overland Company, which produced jeeps for the military, and the Goodyear Aircraft Corporation, which produced airplanes, both prospered during the war. Thanks to the efforts of Ohioans and other Americans, the United States emerged from World War II triumphant."

You could feel the pride of working together for the war effort. You could feel the pain of a lost son, daughter, or father in the war. What a celebration in downtown Toledo when peace was declared first in Germany and then in Japan. Nothing has ever equaled that working together to see our country survive. In our schools, we had paper drives, and we sang the songs of our military, with pride in our voices.

So then the busyness of having a nation prepare for the possibility of being involved in a war they did not want, but when Japan dropped their bombs on Pearl Harbor on December 7, everything changed again. War was a busy time, and moms and dads worked long hours to help the war effort. Home life took on a different look, but there was love and continuity even in this.

We went through all the agony of seeing Germany causing terrible things to happen to the Jews and others they found had no value in their way of looking at things.

Unfortunately, someone like Hitler was able to slowly come into power during the Depression years because Germany was ready to listen to anyone making some sense. But that man brought with him so many hateful ways of destroying what was once so good. So many atrocities happened in so many countries, but we stayed strong as a nation.

When I was fifteen, President Roosevelt died, and there was such sadness. I was on a bike ride with a friend and came home to find this out. President Truman took the reins, and we continued in the war. All this had impact in our family life, but we made it through and found our direction and strength to handle things as they came to us. I have been proud of my parents and saw firsthand what it was like to handle a situation with strength and guidance and always hope.

At that time, the war was almost over when my brother George was sent to Guam as a member of the Navy Seabees and was stationed there. Even though the war was ended, it was dangerous on those islands because there were so many Japanese still in the caves, and they did not know the war was over, and so the military had to be very careful. And how we prayed as a family for his safety. My mom was strong; my father prayed because he remembered too much of his time in France in WWI.

A few extra notes:

When George and Bob were about eight and ten, they were enrolled in our family Methodist Church for their catechism class, but I was too young. However, our wonderful pastor allowed me to go with them, and we sat in his office, just the three of us, and the pastor led us in the learning of the Word. George and Bob had to memorize the verses to be recited in the church services. They did well when the pastor questioned them in the church service about what they had learned. I memorized also, and it was a special time. I remember that, as we walked to church and back, there were unused railroad tracks, and we walked the rails and tried to balance and see how far we could do that. Toledo had many railroad tracks, and at one time, it was considered the railroad center because of the busy route between Chicago and New York. We were also considered the glass city because of the large Owens Corning, Owens Illinois, and Libbey-Owens-Ford that headquartered there. They were a producer of flat glass for automotive and building products. Owens-Corning of Toledo, Ohio, is the world's leading manufacturer of fiberglass and related products. The company got its start during the Great Depression when a company named Owens-Illinois, then a leader in glass product, developed many products in Toledo, Ohio, also.

Our family church held such happy memories for me. This is where I continued to feel God's presence so much, especially in the love of those that attended there. Of course, I was the little Kuehnl girl, and everyone knew the Kuehnls. Most all my aunts and uncles and grandfather from both of my dad and my mom's side belonged there. Considering that my mother and Dad each had about five or more brothers and sisters there. Grandpa taught a men's Wednesday Bible Study.

When I was in class on Sunday, a little elderly man would come in many times, and he would have candy in his pocket and would find a few each Sunday to give a piece to, and I loved it when I was chosen to receive on a few times. The warmth felt in this church has lasted me a lifetime. I was in a two-part play one Sunday evening at church with one of the beautiful Schill daughters, and we were Ruth and Naomi bringing the faithfulness of a daughter-in-law and a mother-in-law to life to show the love they had for one another. Ruth said she would not go back to her own people because she belonged with Naomi, "Wither Thou Goest." I worked very hard on that part. Mother made me practice every chance we could get to do it with "expression." Many times I would be sitting up on the kitchen table next to where Mom was ironing, and we would go over it over and over. She took one part, and I took the other. I remember I was Naomi, and I knew Ruth's lines by heart also and had occasion to whisper a line to her. This church was called Zion Methodist on Segar Street.

Me and boys!

I guess I have to say something about the many boys I liked in the elementary grades. First, there was Harry in the fourth grade that gave me his Aggie. Wow! Harry was playing marbles with a friend as I was walking home from school.

A new school—sixth grade—a note was passed up to me the first day in class: "Who do you think the handsomest boy in the class is?" Signed, Dean. Who is Dean? A note back, "I guess you are." Oh, well!

Early seventh grade—it was Louis who took piano lessons after school and carried his music in a brief case. It was so special. I think I especially liked his quiet demeanor. We talked some times on the telephone, and I liked that a lot! There was Nick in the middle of seventh grade and then Don.

I had three close girlfriends that were very special friends, and we were together a lot. There was Marilyn, Bonnie, and Virginia. Wonderful friends and I wish we would have kept in touch over the years. Bonnie and I have talked on the phone, and we visited her when we were in Northern California a few years ago.

I was growing up and was given opportunities to do things—go ice-skating in a rink and not just on rough outside ice. We did have a lot of nice skating areas outside, and that was fun, even though I had weak ankles, but I also had attached shoe skates to begin with, and they were not great for weak ankles. It was just fun being out with the rest of the kids.

My brothers and I were enrolled in the beautiful Toledo Art Museum, and on most Saturdays, we took the bus and went there for art classes. We also belonged to the Scouts for some time. I don't know how far Bob went, but George almost got his Eagle Scout badge.

I was a good student, but I also liked the social part of growing up. I continued to like school a lot and boys a lot, also.

Then in the eighth grade, I thought this one popular guy was kind of cute, and I told someone about it, and they told him, and before long, he was seeking my attention and continued in high school. Don, a quarterback on the high school team, dances.

As I entered high school, I found that going to dances almost every weekend, it seemed, was wonderful. There was always a live band. The dances were always fun and exciting, and we usually went in a group of six (three with dates—whoever could get their dad's car) and then went out for a hamburger after that.

I was a friend in school that liked everyone—that was just my way and still is. It did not matter if they were very popular or not. They were just friends. No matter who they were, they always had something special about them. I was surprised but proud when I saw in our senior yearbook the caption "wins us all" next to my name. How special that made me feel.

My mother used to ask me after many dances, "Who all did you dance with?" I kept telling her you dance just with the guy you go with. She couldn't get over that. I kidded her that we were not in the days of dance tallies.

I remember weekends—and sometime weeks—at the family cottage at Vineyard Lake in Michigan—the wonderful meals, the guests, the card games, the sunning on the raft, the meeting on the raft of school friends that were at their family cottages, the sitting in the swings in the front yard—contemplating the day, playing badminton, taking long walks after dinner, and then the Sunday drive home after clean-up and closing the cottage, and listening to Jack Benny, Fibber Magee, and Molly and making the little more than an hour trip go by so fast.

Those were good growing-up days, and I enjoyed every minute of these years. Every day made a difference in my life.

During this time as individuals and as a nation, God was always with us; we knew that, but it was a period of time that tested us all and made us stronger or weaker. You chose. Thank goodness, our weak period in my father's life became strong again with a faithful love. So many changes in a ten-year period that changed people, families, and nations.

> "Keep walking with Me along the path I have chosen for you . . . All I require of you is to take the next step, clinging to My hand for strength and direction. Though the path is difficult and the scenery dull at the moment, there are sparkling surprises just around the bend. Stay on the path I have selected for you. It is truly the *path of Life*."
>
> Psalm 16:11

MY MOTHER, JUST A MOM
(And Other Growing-Up Stories)

My mother was thirty-eight when I was born, and by the time of my actual remembrance of her, really looking at her, it probably was about when I was in the third grade. I knew her by what she did and how she lived and what she said but was not conscious of seeing the "outside" of my mother. Perhaps only the inside was what I was focusing on. I did notice she was always tidy and well groomed in her housedresses. She was "just Mom," and I would take her any way she came.

I never knew why she wore her hair in a bun and didn't question it. During the Depression, women didn't go to the beauty parlor to get a permanent. Usually, "during the duration" of this long period of the Great Depression, you didn't spend money on things you could do without because it was something you could sacrifice. So I remember my mother's hair. She had a "bun" in the back of her head. Her hair was very long, and she wrapped it up and twisted it and "anchored" it with hairpins on the nape of her neck.

It was quite a shock when she had her long hair cut and changed to a curly style with a permanent. This came about when things got better after the Depression was working its way out a bit. This would have been about mid-1938. Our parents' main interest was to save so that someday Dad would have enough to start his construction business again. Of course, each family recovered at their own pace. In my husband's family home, their life went on as usual because his father did not lose his position with a company that had work. I didn't know anyone like that, but then I was too young to notice anything but my own surroundings, and others were not talked about. Most people were in the same situation.

My mother, as I was growing up, was much like other mothers—they were quite "matronly" looking. She never had a young look like the mothers of today.

My mother would use the homemaker's dress of the 1940s for her daily appearance with an apron over it. I have to add that she did everything in fairly high heels, but I guess they were comfortable for her. It was not until we had our cottage at Vineyard Lake that I saw my mother in Keds, and she was so little and looked so different to me. This I observed of my mother which I thought was so interesting. Every afternoon, about three, Mom would go up to her bedroom and bathroom to clean up and change into a clean homemaker's dress and with a clean apron over it. She was clean and presentable for Dad and for the family as we gathered together for dinner. The next morning, she put that same outfit on; and again in the afternoon, she changed to a complete clean outfit again. I liked that. She always looked fresh and clean, and I knew why.

Mother did a lot of sewing for us when we were little such as making our snowsuits. And what I loved is that she was always available to us. She loved and cared for her family. She loved her church, and God meant everything to her, and she intimately knew Jesus Christ as her Savior. There was never any doubt of this.

After dinner (or maybe we called it supper), Dad insisted Mom sit down with him after working hard to make a wonderful meal, and we were in teams to do the dishes. When my brothers teamed up, you would want to be out of the house because they were not enjoying their responsibility that much and bantered back and forth. My sister and I were a team, but I fell too many times to agreeing that she would teach me the left hand "chords" on the piano if I would dry the dishes also. She still owes me! She was six years older, and I was her "runner" many times. My sister had an ear for music and could play just by looking at a song sheet of the popular tunes of the day, and I so admired that talent. Never had it myself. I love music but had no talent for any instrument. The only one in the family that played an instrument was George with a trombone. I remember his frequent taking it apart to "release the spit!" Can't remember that he was very good at it, but he practiced. This must have been disappointing to my mother because her family sang and harmonized and enjoyed music in so many ways. Mother never said anything about our lack of this talent; she knew we would have other gifts.

What was so special about my growing up? Radio was a wonderful thing in those days. In my earliest days, I remember the very real-sounding Santa Claus that was on the radio, and we quietly listened to him when he came on about 6:00 p.m. Going to the library was a Saturday event, and I brought home lots of books because I loved to read. The days were long, quiet, and peaceful, and our imagination had time to come into play.

We, as a family, when Dad was working out of town, sat down in the living room with popcorn, turned the radio on, and attentively listened to a wonderful family program called *Those We Love* and other broadcasts of comedians. Earlier in the evening, my brothers had *The Lone Ranger* and other programs. Later, we all enjoyed a radio show called *The Shadow*, and we usually listened to that while in bed. Radio was wonderful. You were not given the picture; you made your own up, and what a special thing that was. Later, we would listen to *Lux Radio Theater* that came on at 9:00

p.m. on Mondays, and many times, Marie and I would listen to that before going to bed.

(When Rol and I married and left Ohio to live in Southern California, we traveled to Hollywood, often to see shows such as *Lux Radio Theater*, *Red Skelton, Groucho Marx, Bing Crosby*, and so many others. What a treat for an Ohio girl. It was so interesting to see how they just read the script, doing *Lux Radio Theater* while holding onto a circular ring or bar while standing up. And they dropped the pages as they finished each page so there would be no noise carried over the airwaves of paper being turned.) Getting back to my young life, this also was my time of "observing" things in life, and that made me quite happy. Maybe this is where my observances were so important to me. My family later said that I could recall things they could not even remember.

Daily interruptions were minimal. In my growing up, there were no cell phones, iPhones, or text messaging to take your mother's attention away from you. The only interruption would be talking to a neighbor or being busy making something wonderful in the kitchen. We had no phone when I was growing up (till the eighth grade), and I didn't know anyone who did. I didn't check it out. It wasn't important.

Mother did the laundry every Monday and hung outside in the summer and hung in the basement in the winter. I helped her in the summer with the laundry—especially the wringer part. This was before a washing machine magically did everything and you did nothing but prepare the clothes and put them in the washer and dryer. Washing machines with wringers—the other "complete kind" that you just put the clothes in, set the dial, put soap in, and shut the door did not come into being until after the war—needed to have clothes put in the hot water in the tub of the washer, swish back and forth with an agitator many times, and then Mother knew when it was time to put them through the process of this wringer that would then roll the clothes through to get most of the water out and then comes one rinse, wringer again, and then another rinse and wringer. Finally, that load is ready to be hung. An all-day event.

We had six of us in the family—but then we didn't have that many clothes, and we wore them more than once—but the basket was always full to overflowing. Another few loads that Mother always had were the sheets for all the beds. I was always amazed at my mother on "wash" day. She had time, in between loads, to come up to the kitchen to make a beautiful pie for dinner. What a treat. On Tuesdays, she always ironed—all day! And the week went on with cleaning, sweeping outside/inside, and all the chores with housekeeping that she did willingly and lovingly. And what a cook my mother was. Beautiful meals, many times simple during the Depression—good stuff like macaroni and cheese, homemade baked beans in a bean crock, and homemade catsup with cornbread. Dad liked to enter into the kitchen and cook or help also, and he would say, for effect, once in a while, "I taught her all she knows!" She let that go, but it was all in fun. Dad's input was to sneak a bud of garlic into Sunday's beef roast, and we had pleaded beforehand. "Dad, no garlic." Someone always got the piece that was strong with garlic, and he had to take the consequences of unhappy kids.

Once, when Mother was making a big pot of vegetable soup chock-full of good things, someone looked at it while it was cooking and asked, "What is all that foamy white stuff floating on the top of the soup?" Mr. Innocence didn't say anything, but it was soon learned that he found a lonely apple in the refrigerator and peeled it and cut it up and threw it in the soup. These were fun family times, things you remember.

I remember how I loved to bake when I was growing up, and one time, because I loved apricot pie, my mom had gone downtown on errands.

(Everything was "downtown" in those days until they started building small satellite shopping centers all over—taking the bus downtown was a big thing and lots of fun.) So I was just finished with taking the pie out of the oven, and my dad came into the kitchen and sat on the stepping stool. I asked him if he would like a piece, and he said, "Of course."

He was my best critic because he always praised what I did. I cut the piece and saw that it was quite sticky but pretty. (I guess I had put too much thickening in it.) Dad sat there and ate this thick, sticky apricot pie, and his comment to me was, "It has a wonderful flavor, honey." Oh, that was a great compliment without direction. I guess that was what our family was all about. You discovered on your own what you could do and always were appreciated for trying. Happy remembrances.

Dad was always a good storyteller, and we, sometimes, heard the same story, but he would embellish it, and it was wonderful hearing him tell it again. Many times, if company was over, we sat at his feet so as to hear everything.

In the summer, my father was one to be out in the countryside during his work schedule with construction, and he brought home bushel baskets full of tomatoes and anything else that could be canned. Many times Mom just got finished with one bushel basket of something, and Dad would bring home another. After my father died, when I was nineteen, she said, "No more mason jars and fruit cellar for me," and she meant it. She never canned again. The fruit cellar lived on with cobwebs, and old mason jars lined up with nothing in them.

Whenever we would take a drive or had to be somewhere, it was understood that Dad would take us to the car after we were all ready and would sit in the car in the driveway, and we would give that time for Mom to get ready. I thought that was great. It served another purpose; we stayed clean during the wait instead of running around and getting dirty.

I remember Mom telling how she had gotten my two brothers ready for Sunday school and got ready herself for church, and when she needed them to come so we could go, Bob came home with his white trousers all dirty. You didn't want to put Bob in white, ever!

My mother was so special in my eyes. She never scolded but did expect us to be obedient and use good judgment. I've said this before; none of us would do a thing to hurt her because her goodness and example was just there to follow. One of the things I can say about her is she did not do everything for us; she let us choose our own road. It was an easy choice because she was the example for living life right and making good choices.

We loved our mother and father very much, and aside from the fact we had some down times when my father drank "with his working buddies," home was a special place. Both my mother and father had a sense of humor in their response to things, and I loved that.

Simple memories of growing up but wonderful at the same time.

"With skillful hands he led them."

Psalm 78:72

"When you are unsure which course to take, totally submit your own judgment to that of the Spirit of God, asking Him to shut every door except the right one. But meanwhile, keep moving ahead and consider the absence of a direct indication from God to be the evidence of His will that you are on His path. And as you continue down the long road, you will find that He has gone before you, locking doors you otherwise would have been inclined to enter. Yet you can be sure that somewhere beyond the locked doors is one He has left unlocked. And when you open it and walk through, you will find yourself face to face with a turn in the river of opportunity—one that is broader and deeper than anything you ever dared to imagine, even in your wildest dreams. So set sail on it because it flows to the open sea." (Horace Bushnell)

"Test me in this . . . and see if I will not throw open the floodgates of heaven and pour out so much blessing that you will not have room enough for it."

Malachi 3:10

Here is what God is saying in this verse. "My dear child, I still have floodgates in heaven, and they are still in service. The locks open as easily as before, and the hinges have not grown rusty. In fact, I would rather throw them open to pour out the blessings than hold them back. I opened them for Moses, and the sea parted. I opened them for Joshua, and the Jordan River was stopped. I opened them for Gideon, and the armies of the enemy fled. And I will open them for you—*if you will only let me.*"

(John Henry Jowett)

More growing up memories . . .

Before we had refrigeration, we had ice boxes—probably had them invented, but because of the Depression, they didn't sell many. So this was in our kitchen, and in the front room window, we had the sign that (top number) indicates how big a piece of ice the ice man needs to bring in through the back door and place it in the ice box. It was fun to see him stop at every house, open up his ice truck, and get out his heavy gloves and his ice pick and his ice tongs. He would then throw the ice block over his shoulder, enter the back door, open up the ice section of the ice box, and fit the ice in. Sometimes, he had to use his ice pick to get it just right. I am not quite sure, but I think this would be a weekly delivery.

Additionally, in Ohio, many people had kitchen "window boxes" in the winter time and placed butter or such in those boxes because they kept very cold. Extra storage in the winter for a big family.

When refrigerators were manufactured, our family bought one, and it was wonderful. One of our first modern conveniences, and I am sure my mother loved it. We had to place it in the large dining room till the ice box was removed, and I went into that room many times to open this fascinating appliance, and upon opening it, the light would come on. What a wonder.

Ice houses still existed for some things, but I suppose the ice man lost his job. This was a time of modern things taking over and jobs eliminated, and it goes on yet, only faster.

The milk man delivered milk according to what Mother put in a note in the bottle. We loved to get up in the morning in the winter and gather in the milk bottles because the cream at the top pushed the cap way up, and the cream became frozen. Was that ever good! Mother said that Babcock Dairy, who delivered milk to our home during the Depression, continued to deliver even if Mother could not pay that week because she had been such a good customer—four children—and he did not have the heart to see us go without milk. Compassion.

Our mailman, Charlie, delivered mail twice a day, Monday through Saturday and during Christmas time, once on Sunday (after the Depression, and people could afford to send their Christmas cards out again). He had to trudge through the snow, slush, ice, and then summer heat twice a day but was always cheery about it. I can still see Charlie's face in my mind's eye. A sweet man who seemed to love what he was doing.

The jukebox—when we got to be teenagers, and things were doing better, every hamburger joint had a jukebox, and we would (someone who had a quarter would) put a quarter in, and we would hear the latest music. You chose what song you wanted to hear.

Telephones—all different shapes, and during the war, we had "party lines." More than one family shared a line, and you had to listen for your ring and also hope the other parties don't talk too long—it could be as many as four to six families sharing a line. (As a rule, we never had any trouble because we used it only as needed, and I think the others respected that also.) We did not have one during the Depression, and most people did not. We did not get a phone until about 1940. No one missed it, but it was important when I started higher grades, and boys called!

Grocery shopping—before 1941. We had to go to a little neighborhood store and give them a store list to fill. You usually wait your turn until they filled it, bagged it, and then wrote up the individual bill, and you paid for it. Never would work today. It took a long time to wait till they got to you because they had to fill each order, and it included the meat market also. When my mother sent me to a corner store, she always said, "Now, don't let Ernie give you fatty pork chops just because you are a child." I used to watch carefully and would lean down to see his hands in the meat case and pick out the pork chops, and I learned a lesson on how to shop!

An evening with lollipops. We were sitting on the front porch on a summer's evening, and my dad said, "Let's have a lollipop." Father would give me six cents, and I would take orders from everyone on what flavor they wanted, and I would run to the corner drugstore to get the lollipops for a simple but good family time. My preference was hot cinnamon. Just enjoying this time together. Worth more than a penny in memory! We were used to the simple things, and that was one of the special times.

Gas stations were funny things—usually small—and they had two or three young men that came out to check your oil/water levels and to do the windows—while filling the tank. Sometimes, they all would come out running, and it was always fun to see.

We had three large sour cherry trees in our backyard, and when the war was on, and my brothers were busy with some way to help the war effort in jobs available to them. So my dad had put me to the task of climbing a ladder (which I always felt unsure on), and I was not a happy girl. I did not like climbing trees, and I did not like being high on ladders. I survived the best I could, but I am not sure how. They certainly were not all picked. Then Mom and I would pit them, and I would help her can them. These must have been my "Martha" years. I was so glad when Dad planned a summer vacation to a favorite lake in Michigan, and the birds got the cherries while we were gone. It was the first thing I looked at when arriving home. I think Dad might have planned that with me in mind. My father used to say, "Someday you will think back at these wonderful cherries, and when you eat a cherry pie, you will remember this." I said, "No way," but he was right. And it happens to be my husband's favorite pie.

My father loved being a good provider for his family and bought in large quantities.

World War II

Ration books during the war.

It was announced in the paper how to use the books and where to apply for additional books, if approved. We all got acquainted with the ration books, and we were limited on so many things: sugar and all household food and then also gasoline. You only got what you needed to get you to work and back and not much else. Gasoline was very limited to help with the war effort. So many things were no longer available.

Foodstuffs like bananas were scarce; and many things including sugar, meat, butter, cheese, eggs, milk, tea, chocolate, clothes, fuel oil, rubber, typewriters, and cooking oil were rationed. This happened because the Nazis were sinking ships importing these foods and materials (Internet).

Nearly all food products were rationed. Cloth, wood, and metal, as well as rubber and leather, were all rationed so that the armed forces would have enough for their needs.

Gasoline, oil, and grease, as well as kerosene and industrial alcohol and ink. Paper, carbon paper, pencils, pens, and typewriter ribbons, as well as erasers and paper clips and envelopes.

Automobile tires, parts, and belts were all unavailable during the war as the factories were sending all their production to the military's needs. Nylon and silk were used for parachutes, not women's stockings (Internet). It seemed everyone knew how to use a patch kit to repair their tire inner tubes again and again.

These inconveniences you get used to because everyone was affected, and also, we were all proud to help in the war effort.

Most homes, I believe, were heated with coal. Every year, Mother and Dad would gauge how much they would need and then put the order in. The big coal truck would arrive with a chute he put in the basement window to go directly into the coal bin and fill it up so we would be warm and toasty in the winter. I was always amused that it was my mother that went down to fill the furnace to start the fire, and soon, the warm heat would fill the house. I guess she didn't mind, and it started our day.

Then houses converted to gas or oil. We had a register where the heat came up to heat everything, and once we had a radiator, and that was fun because when I came in from play or school, I would take a pillow over to the register, climb up, and read. My husband asked how I ever grew up in cold Ohio when I prefer the warmth of a sunny climate. I told him I even ate my bowl of ice cream standing on the register.

Baths—once a week if you needed them or not—to have hot water in our home anyway; the water heater was lighted by Mom when she went down to the water heater in the basement and open the little grate and put a match to the pilot light, and it would start the heater to heat the water that was needed for the Saturday night bath. After it was lighted, it took about half an hour to get the water hot enough to fill the bathtub once. It was turned off once the tub was filled. Now comes the hard part. Mom would announce the bath water was ready and who wanted to go first. Nobody rushed to say "me." So with a little persuasion, we would each stop what we were doing and climb into the tub. The purpose of this story is to say if you wait too long, you get the last of the bath water, and it could be pretty dirty if you followed my brothers.

Having just one bathroom in a two-story, three-bedroom home was the usual, and it always seemed to work around six people in the family. Sometimes, you just waited outside the door to the bathroom and keep announcing, "hurry, hurry."

A story that comes to mind regarding standing on the register. When I was about in the third grade, I did not go right home but stopped and played with a school friend that lived on my way home. I was there for about an hour. I walked home and opened the front door, and my brothers and sister were sitting in the living room, and Mom was standing up by the register. I had not told anyone what I was doing after school, and everyone was concerned. I was so surprised to see them all there, and I can say that I never did that again. Mother talked to me and said that I just cannot do that unless telling her. It was another lesson learned.

We had many destinations, and you did not have to drive very far out of Toledo to be in the farm area. We used to visit relatives in Swanton, Ohio, and also an aunt and uncle in Metamora, Ohio. They were both fun to visit. The Swanton relatives had a farm with a long drive to the farm house, and it was rutted and just dirt. At the end was a good visit, and we enjoyed it so much.

Ruth, a cousin there, asked me to stay for a week one time, and this city girl was out of her area of comfort. I didn't want to go to the outhouse at night, so my aunt put a bed pan under the bed for me. Security! And one day, my uncle asked if we would dig up potatoes in one area. Who knew potatoes grew under the ground! Surprise. Dirty job, but we did it. I had taken a swim suit. Am I kidding? Where is there a water hole? We had two on a bike going into town one day, and that was quite a long bike ride but such fun, and at the end, we stopped by my uncle's work, and he gave us money to have a Sundae. Great stuff.

I was also invited one time for Halloween, and it was so beautiful with the full moon, the stalks showing in the shadows of the night, and the distances between houses that a city girl thought long. Every house knew my cousin and asked us in, so we had a little chat at almost every house.

School days—walking to school after ice storms, and it was hard to walk on the sidewalk or grass. No one ever could come after us or take us if it was raining hard or snowing or ice. You just walked the distance. There was only one car in the family, and Dad had that for work. Once, Dad was home at lunch time and gave me five cents to get a treat at a corner store as I walked to school. A Clark bar, a favorite, made the walk so much more delightful.

When Dad was home, he was the one who listened to the radio news early in the morning, and when the weather was real bad, they would announce which schools would be closed that day, and then Dad would come into each bedroom and say, "No school today." What great words to hear! We could stay in that warm bed, and it was special. And it was so beautiful, peaceful, and quiet looking out the window and seeing winter perform its lustrous beauty.

We didn't go out to eat as a family because most of our growing up was in the Depression times. And besides that, Mom was such a good cook. So it was a new thing for me to go out for hamburgers after a date and then a wonderful thing when I met my husband-to-be, and he took me out "to dine." Made a big impression.

I remember, before the ration books came out in wartime, my father went to the meat market and got six large porterhouse steaks, and we had a marvelous steak dinner on Sunday to recognize the fact that this would not be possible again until after the war. And it wasn't.

I spent a lot of time taking out books from the library all my life, and that had been special. I loved the walks there and back. And the feeling that my arms carried stories to fill my mind with new memories to carry me away to another time or another way of life was full of anticipation.

Sunday family drives were a ritual in most families, it seemed. Fun when you were younger with the famous hot dog with chili at the end of the drive or an ice cream cone, but I think it was a big disappointment to my father when we got older and didn't want to take that family drive. I think it meant a lot to him and hard to give up.

My mother and dad had a little ritual every four years at election time. On voting day, my mother would be going out the door to walk to the local church or school to vote, and my father would say (he was a Democrat; she was a Republican), "Don't forget how you should vote," and she would answer back, "You will never know, will you?"

And I remember when it was a shock when voters went to bed thinking Thomas Dewey, the presidential candidate, had won but in the morning found out Harry S. Truman, the Democrat, won. (News traveled very slow—in the daytime, paperboys would shout in the neighborhood "Extras" so people could hear and go out and get the latest news. Seems so funny now with the advent of CNN and the like with twenty-four-hour news.)

On many Sundays, we would visit my grandfather and aunt. My grandfather had a shoe shop in the rear side of the garage and fixed shoes. Years and years before he made the shoes from scratch, and that was a talent. When my brothers and I would go visit him, we would see all those old-fashioned shoe molds made of wood in different sizes and his sewing machine and would smell the leather, shoe polish, and the many other things he had from days gone by. It was always interesting. He would be there, and we knew he had his little muffin tin of change right there by the sewing machine, and before we left the shop, he would give each of us a dime. He was a sweet grandfather.

Toledo had a lot of different mixtures of people from all over the world. On the north side were the Lebanese, the east side, the Hungarians and Polish, the south side and west end (and I lived in both areas) were usually white Anglo-Saxon but not all Protestant. Toledo had many Catholics, a pretty big Jewish population and a bit of black.

Often, on Sunday at 4:00 p.m., my father and some of us would drive down to Canton Avenue and pick up the most delicious Jewish rye and pumpernickel bread just out of the oven. What a treat to go with the left-over beef roast from the middle of the day dinner.

When I was growing up—and I don't think I was too different than many families—I seemed to get all my cousin Jeanette's hand-me-downs, and usually, they were not a style that appealed to me, but I wore them anyway and was content. It was a great surprise when things got better with Dad working regularly with the WPA, that Mom came home from downtown with a new dress for me. I kept telling her, "Mom, Mom, you didn't tell me that you were getting me a new dress." How I loved that dress.

I remember Christmas. There were a few years we especially remember because our parents told us to choose one thing that we would really like to receive on Christmas. This took a lot of thought, but one Christmas, when I was in the fourth grade, I told my parents that I would love to have my own purse, and my mother bought me one that was brown and opened on both sides, and I just loved it and pretended such fun things as I assembled things in it to "organize" it. Santa wasn't the one who brought things for a few years. Just Mom and Dad. But how happy we were with less.

New shoes were not often purchased, except for size change. My father had a kit (lots of kits during those days) that fixed the sole of the shoe. It had rubber soles and glue, and it was fun to watch as Dad put on another layer to an old sole. It was okay, I guess, maybe a bit to get used to, but we did it with no complaints.

The Depression was probably hard for parents, but kids grew up just enjoying life, and that is what we did.

I don't know if all states did this during the war, but Ohio had a visiting nurse come out to a home when a member of the family had some communicable disease. She would make her determination and take care of the patient and leave instructions and then tack up the sign before leaving. I remember walking to school in our early days and going past houses of friends with "Quarantine" signs on and knew we would not see them for a while.

As I remember, Father had to find a place to stay for a few days so he would not take it out of the house.

There were many hot summer days that our father took us to Maumee River to have fun in the water close to the shore. I would sit on Dad's shoulders like all young kids do, and it was fun. However, that stopped when the river was tested, and the epidemic of polio was rampant. No longer could we do that. I had a friend in high school that had a severe case of polio before we ever had the Salk vaccines and was very paralyzed. Susan, regardless, made herself a very successful life and got many degrees and taught in one of the colleges in California.

And the many parks in Toledo were wonderful when the family had picnics or watched the fireworks. Such lovely memories.

George, one time, picked up a firecracker that he thought was a dud, but it blew up in his hand, and he had quite a bad burn. Another picnic, I asked Dad to throw me a peach, and it went a little over my head, and I leaned back to try to get it, and my elbow hit hard on an end of a soda bottle that was broken. Another picnic ruined. It was usually Bob that needed attention, but George and I got our time in that also.

Quiet Sabbaths—why was that hard? The whole house went quiet. First, Sunday school and sometimes stayed for church, middle of the day dinner on Sunday, naps and rest time, a quiet family drive, and then a lovely family supper. It dragged to me, but we observed the Sabbath. Sometimes, there was church music in the afternoon from the radio. Even though our life was not harried, it was hard to slow down more.

History has always been so interesting to me. Mainly U.S. history: the Revolutionary War, the Civil War, World War I—because my dad was in it—and World War II because it was such a part of my growing-up years.

I always loved school, and it got more and more interesting to me with dances in the school gym. Got bawled out by the dreaded science teacher though once because she thought I danced with one boy too much. Never thought I did. That was in the eighth grade and a new activity at our school. Glad Mom didn't find out that I got bawled out. I have often wondered about this. It was such a surprise to me that she stopped our dancing and said these things. She was a teacher I could not understand, and I tried. My rationalization was that she liked boys better than girls. She didn't have anything to say to the boys I was dancing with.

A change in history that changed so much.

December 7, 1941, was a sad day. Pearl Harbor was attacked, and the next day, President Roosevelt declared war on Germany and Japan. We woke up early on a Sunday, and our life changed forever. The radio news was on often, and my father kept very informed. Things changed a good deal. I was eleven and in the seventh grade, I believe. I was growing up and having an opening up in my own mind, but the world was opening up also. Living through wartimes like that in World War II was different because it involved everyone. There were new things to get used to, but we did it, willingly. Each day brought something new and made us grow up with a lot of knowledge of what was going on. We learned to do without and be proud of it.

When President Roosevelt died in 1945, the whole nation mourned. To me, I felt like he was a strong father-figure to our country. It was a sad time.

I was never as happy as when I started sixth grade. I loved my new school, McKinley, in the west end of Toledo. I had many new friends, and I had a tremendous "liberated" feeling because I was feeling "grown up," and that felt so good. It just was the beginning of so much growth in me that wanted to come out in so many ways. I felt good; I felt different. The world was changing; I was changing.

My Mother and me the day of Dolores and Bob's Wedding,
July 14, 1951

ABOUT MY DEAR FATHER
George Edward Kuehnl

I loved him, and I look forward to seeing and being with him (and my dear mother) again someday.

His mother died when he was nine. His father remarried a wonderful

woman that was loved by him and all of us. They had five more children, and my father and his two sisters were very much always part of the family. I know my father drew strength from the faith that was in the family life he had.

He joined the army before WWI ever began. The first correspondence I have in my possession would make him twenty-two when he was stationed in Fort Sam Houston,

Texas, in 1916, and the letter his father wrote to General Pershing's office states he joined in May 1916 when he ran away from home and enlisted in the army. The attached letter is to his father and one from his father to, probably, his commanding officer. His father stated, in essence, he was needed at home to help with the grocery store and home responsibilities. The answer was that "he could apply to the Secretary of War and state 'through patriotic reasons, your son ran away, and we learned from George that he is thoroughly penitent for having left home.'"

Formerly, men were allowed to purchase their discharge from the service, but owing to the Mexican trouble, this privilege has been denied them—they stated, "It would cost your son, George, one hundred and twenty dollars," and his father answered, "He has the money, but the commanding office will not let him apply.

"Because of failing health (his father's), you need his services at home, also ask for information as how to get him discharged—he will, in all probability, be furloughed to the Army Reserve, allowed to return home but of course, would be subject to call in the event of actual hostilities which, let us hope, never happens. You can use your own judgment in this matter."

In the letter to the office of General Pershing, commander in chief of the U.S. Army in France, April 4, 1919 (attached), my father's father wrote, "I wish to say my son, George E. Kuehnl, *enlisted at the time when the Mexican troubles started in the year 1916 in the month of May.*" He also mentioned that "both of them had the wish to have him help our country."

His father continues in the same letter, "From San Antonio, Texas, the government took him to Europe and stayed there since the trouble started in service and is at present in Hillsheid, near Coblenz. He enrolled in their Army of Occupation Field Hospital #13 APO 729." He was there through the duration of the war. The government had sent him to Europe until the trouble started with WWI and was stationed some of the time in Hillsheid, near Coblenz. Dad wrote on a long map of the Rhine and surrounding areas, "I made the trip down the Rhine as far as Bonn. A very nice boat ride. And a few days ago, I was in

Coblenz, so I spent the day taking in a trip up the Rhine. To read this map right, Koln (Cologne) is where the English are, and that is what we call down the Rhine.

Coblenz (or Koblenz, west Central Germany, southeast of Bonn) is our place, and Mainz (upriver from Frankfurt on the Main River) is where the French are, and that is up the Rhine—written March 30, 1919."

My father was with the first division. He enrolled in their Army of Occupation Field Hospital #13 APO 729 and served as an ambulance driver that drove to the front lines to pick up the dead and injured and took them to the field hospital.

The war was ended by several treaties, most notably the Treaty of Versailles, signed on June 28, 1919, although the allied powers had an armistice with Germany in place since November 11, 1918. One of the most striking results of the war was a large redrawing of the map of Europe. All of the Central Powers lost territory, and many new nations were created. The German empire lost its colonial possessions and was saddled with accepting blame for the war as well as paying punitive reparations for it. The Austro-Hungarian and Ottoman empires were completely dissolved.

Austria-Hungary was carved up into several successor states including Austria, Hungary, Czechoslovakia, and Yugoslavia.

In his letter, his father goes on to add that they would be thankful for his release—his father died in Toledo in 1923 at sixty-one years of age and is buried in Forest Cemetery—and send him home to assist him and the family. He continues, "As far as we know, all the trouble is over, and you could spare him from the honorable work and help he has done in our estimation for our country."

My father returned home from the WWI and his service in France July 2, 1919.

My father was born on September 9, 1894, in Portland, Oregon.
He died on December 7, 1949, at the age fifty-five.
(Coronary Thrombosis) in Toledo, Ohio. (Toledo Hospital)

Attached: Germany's tribute to the First Division

COPY OF ATTACHED LETTER (the letter regarding German thoughts regarding the First Division.

Headquarters First Division
American E.F.
October 10, 1918

GERMANY'S TRIBUTE TO THE FIRST DIVISION

Today a captured Colonel of the German Army arrived at our division cage. He was cold, hungry and broken in spirit. After four years of severe fighting and constant service in his army, he was taken prisoner by the victorious troops of the First Division.

The following is the substance of his remarks:

"Yesterday I received orders to hold the ground at all costs. The American barrage advanced toward my position and the work of your artillery was marvelous. The barrage was so dense that it was impossible for us to move out of our dugouts. Following this barrage closely were the troops of the First Division. I saw them forge ahead and knew that all was lost. All night I remained in my dugout, hoping vainly that something would happen that would permit me to rejoin my army. This morning your troops found me and here I am, after four years of fighting, a prisoner."

"Yesterday I knew that the First Division was opposite us, and I knew that we would have to put up the hardest fight of the war. The First Division is wonderful and the German Army knows it. We did not believe that within five years the Americans could develop such a division as the First Division. The work of its infantry and artillery is worthy of the best armies in the world."

(I could not read some of the following about this Tribute but I can read this "It is with the greatest pleasure that we learn that even our enemies recognize the courage, valor and efficiency of our troops. The work done by the First Division during the past few days will go down in history as one of those memorable events which will live in the hearts of the American people for generations to come.

Every member of this command deserves the enthusiastic congratulations from, and the high respect in which it is held by our comrades in arms and by the entire American nation.

The above will be published to every member of this Command.

By Command of Major General Summerall

COPY OF ATTACHED LETTER (little hard to read but I love it because it is in my Father's handwriting)- original in Binder Six)

October, 1918 - France

My dear Father,

Received a letter from Bertha Klotz and she stated that you were in an accident. I hope you were not hurt very bad. What was the trouble. Did Nellie run away with you! I got a hard lump on my head a few days ago. You know I am driving a three tone truck since the Field Hospital had to turn in their (towing or touring) car. I was about 50 miles away from the Co. and one of my springs worked out of place. So I got the jack and my tools and had it jacked up and the whole works dropped down on me. But I am all ok except a sore forehead. But if that is all I get out of this war I am a good one. I forgot to tell you I got it all fixed up and am out at work hauling every day and some times even at night. The weather is getting bad. I hate to have to put this winter in, as the last one was very bad. The mud is up to my ankles but otherwise I think every thing is going first (rate/straight??) We still have the Germans on the way to Berlin. This spring I look for a world's peace. I wish it would come this winter but it doesn't look like it yet. But a fellow never can tell. Things happen very often. I am enclosing a little note of German's tribute to the Division. This is what the German's think of us so don't you think we are on the job?

Your Loving Son, George

Chauffeur G.E. Kuehnl
Field Hosp. 13 A.P.O. 729
American E F

(note: this is partially censored and then initialed by the censor at the bottom of the letter - I thought it would be a better way to decipher this letter if I typed what I thought it said - rl)

All the letters my Father wrote showed the love he had for his Father and family.

My Father was an ambulance driver that had to drive to the front lines to pick up injured soldiers and take them to the Field Hospital - dangerous work

There are so many things I want to say about my dear Father. He was brave, he was good, he was a good brother and husband and father. He came from a loving family and that gave him the groundwork to become such a good man who loved the Lord. I have always been proud of him.

OUR DEAR FAMILY
About 1930

Brother Bob, our dad, Brother George on other knee.

Mom has the girls—little me, probably six to eight months old, and Marie, about seven.

We are in front of our home on Glenn Court—all dressed up and looking so good. Wonder what kind of a story is behind the getting ready and staying clean! Anyway, it worked, and I have this picture. I love this picture.

Ruth Carolyn Kuehnl Lampe

God is always faithful, always

In his time of difficulty in his life,
my father's weakness drove us all down the Road to Calvary
because we saw living like that was not for us,
and that was made clear.

THE GIFT OF MY MOTHER IN MY LIFE

How can I ever explain this wonderful, loving, special mother that I have always loved so much and shaped my life in the strong belief in God I have always had?

She loved, each of us, unconditionally—without judgment or harsh words did we ever hear from her. She did not discipline; she lived and showed us by how she lived how living is done. There was *never* a time we did not know where she got her strength. She believed and leaned on God so heavily that we could "feel it" without words.

I never remember my mother, once, raising her voice or getting mad at me or any of us. That just was not her nature. That just was not how she saw life should be lived. There was something about her that gave us confidence in ourselves.

Mom had never complained about things that needed to be done or responsibilities that were too heavy. She quietly expected the best from us, just as God expects the best in each of us.

Her strengths from being raised in a godly family gave her strengths for life that she passed on. Whoever you would talk to, they would say, "She is so special!" You could *never* put your finger on it. She just was there, available and loving. Never did she judge others or make remarks that were unkind of others. What was it, Mother, what made you so different? It was God, wasn't it?

My father, who we all loved, gave us pain at times, but my mother always taught us respect for him because we knew he had a weakness for drinking that made him a different person at times, and we have some hard memories that we carry, but he loved us so much, and in the best of times, he was there, and his love was there, and we drew strength from that. Why did he start drinking?

From being a half-brother and sharing his father and losing his birth mother at nine—but yet still have so much love for his stepmother. Was it what he saw in WWI carrying very injured or dead bodies from the front lines in his job as ambulance driver in France? Was it his work in the field of the building business that gave him too many temptations with others that drank? Who knows? Only God. I know he was sorry for it. That was enough. My mother understood; we understood. Forgiveness was always a big part of our family life, and life went on.

I loved my mother so much and will always love her. She is my reason for being the person I am, the one striving to be a follower of the Lord with all my heart. I follow my mother down that road, and I thank her for her constant love and for giving me a life that gave me such strengths.

Thank you, dear Mom. We will be together again. I love you. Your daughter, Ruth

This is our Mother

The difficult circumstances in life and the times of waiting often refine, teach, and prepare us for the future responsibilities God has for us.

Mother, you have instilled in us the precious values in life. You gave us all the instruction we needed for life, just by the way you led your life and we always knew who led you.

Our Mother is sitting in the chair and area in the living room where she would go to meet the Lord in her study of The Word and her time with

Him. They communicated and she got her strength in her strong belief and faith.

This, in her time of devotions, is indelible in my memory. We knew this was her time with Him and we were quiet when we approached this sanctuary that she had. Mother and God communicated and she got her strength in her strong belief and strength.

MORE REMEMBRANCES OF OUR MOM AND DAD

Mom never scolded but did expect us to be obedient and use good judgment. I've said this before; none of us would do a thing to hurt her because her goodness and example was just there to follow. One of the things I can say about her is she did not do everything for us; she let us choose our own road. It was an easy choice because she was the example for living life right and making good choices.

My father was a wonderful storyteller, and when we had company, we would almost sit at his feet to hear this story told once again with elaboration and in his style because he made it so interesting. They loved us and showed it in so many ways.

CHILDHOOD MEMORIES

I remember having our mother call us to the kitchen door and giving out pieces of bubble gum and turning to me and saying, "Let's share the last piece." She did not think I should have the full piece—being so little. This is how fair she always was, and I was glad to share with my mother, and I think she handled it well.

I remember parts of our house very well, especially the kitchen, sitting room, and side door to kitchen.

Mother mentioned about my brother Bob going through the same field George did and if there was a piece of glass, Bob would somehow fall on it and get cut. I would have to say that we would call Bob 'adventurous'.

ICE TONGS
A great attraction for kids as they watch for the iceman as he delivers to homes, waiting to get some chips that fall as he prepares a block of ice to carry into the. He adjusts his ice tongs around the block and carries it around the house to the back door and puts it in the ice box.

This a German-made cherry pitter – the very likeness of the one Mom and I used after I picked the cherries on the 3 trees, went in the kitchen to help Mom pit the cherries and then we prepared the mason jars to can them

This pitter automatically lifts the cherry and drops it into your bowl. Since the cherries come out whole and virtually undamaged with only a small hole in its center, it gives Cherries for prize-winning pies. This pitter works great for sour cherries.

This is just like the washing machines that all Mothers used .

Wringer washers can save money on water, heating and electricity costs. A typical washing machine uses 40 gallons of water to fill the tub for one load. It also uses another 40 gallons of water to wash three loads rinsing is the same. So three loads of wash would use a total of 80 gallons of water, as compared to 240 gallons of water for three washes in a typical washing machine.

Wringer washers use less energy, too. A wringer washer can be set to run for as long as you like. For normal clothing, wash for 9-15 minutes. Heavily soiled loads can go a bit longer. Compare that for 30-45 minutes with a typical washer from start to finish, depending on the settings. You can find wringer washers that run on propane gas or wringer washers that run on manual power using a crank. The crank is a lot of work, but if you are interested in not using any purchased

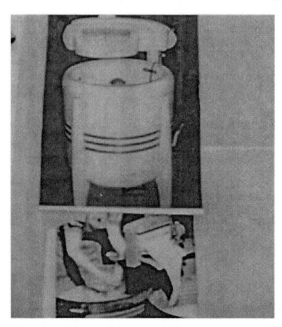

energy, it is a good choice. (This was written during the depression when you watched costs of everything – my Mother's machine did not use a crank, thank goodness.

Wringer washings can use less laundry detergent too. The increased agitation of the wringer gets everything very cleans with just a bit of detergent.) (Internet)

I remember at Grandpa's house, we played hide-and-go-seek. I think everyone could relate to playing hide-and-go-seek into the dusk of the evening. I recall that I was quite little and seemed excited to hide, but no one ever thought me part of the game. I couldn't run fast enough, never hid very far from the start, but watching the others so excited seem to bring a lot of happiness to me.

Mother walking us to school and returned for us later—and at lunch time. She walked that distance four times a day with Bootsy, our dog.

I remember Mom made root beer and stored it up in the unfinished attic and said it had to age so we would not drink it so fast. Said it had to "age." George said much later, "Doubt it."

Some special memories that a lot of us would remember.

Picture of me in sixth grade

TWO BROTHERS AND A LITTLE SISTER!

And another sister, Marie, who was our cousin that my family raised when her mother died when she was six weeks old.

Families are so important, and living together, growing up brings back so many memories that bring joy and smiles as you look back over the years.

My brothers are both gone now, and my sister is not well. How soon that happened. Except for my sister, who was six years older than me, we were born within three and a half years of one another and were always close. They were special brothers, and we had a special bond. Marie, being six years older than me, was on a wavelength all her own, and we were not terribly alike. We had to room together in the same bedroom, but other than meals and doing dinner dishes, we didn't have things to do together.

I remember when Mother would take the bus to go downtown on a Saturday. This was after Mom and Marie had cleaned the house, and Marie was left with us. I remember many times when she would chase us upstairs with a broom to keep the downstairs clean, and we would run like we could not run fast enough, and this happened over and over because it was fun getting her ire up.

George, the oldest, and then Bob, the middle child, were tremendously close as brothers, all their life. They, after my father's death in 1949, took over my father's construction business when they were just in their very early twenties, and they worked it and held on to it till they had more experience and jobs acquired because they kept up the same honest integrity that my father had, and people believed in them and their work.

They both had a natural talent for this work, and it came to them easily. George was the businessman keeping ahead of the jobs, and eventually, they went from small business construction to very large buildings. Bob was in charge of the men on the jobs and was known to be a perfectionist, and a nephew shared, while working for Uncle Bob when he was growing up, that Bob did not throw a thing away, and young George had to straighten nails so they could be used and not thrown out. We enjoyed hearing that story.

Growing-up stories involved many times just watching them enjoy being together, whether it was two on their used bike pedaling off somewhere or adventuring in the many open fields we had growing up.

It was special when I could be a part of their life, and when Bob had a Sunday paper route—in the dead of winter—I would sometimes go out with him very early in the morning when it was still dark, using the sled to pull the papers—and keeping him company in bitter cold weather.

George was in every way my older brother. He saw things he didn't like and would tell me about them, whether it was a boyfriend he thought should not drive me or be with any longer. He always told me how nice I looked and dressed, and I could always tell he was proud of me. Before I got into high school and George had already been there two years, he had told so many girls in his homeroom, "Just wait till my little sister gets here." He was that proud, and they told me about it when I got there, and I was pleased. George had a temperament like my mother and was quiet and never argumentative. He did not like arguments.

We were the generation of families that sat down at every meal together, and that includes a lot of memories. My father knew I loved the breast of chicken and saw to it I always got it—and that seemed to be OK with everyone—until after my father died when I was nineteen, and at family dinner on Sundays, my new sister-in-law loved the breast also, and I had to give that up—I forgot who got the other half—and did I ever miss my father at that time. But these are lessons in learning to share—not sure I overcame that!

IT WAS THE PITS

It was about 1942, and I was twelve.

We were in the war years, and many families were involved for long hours working for the war effort. It was no different for us. My father and brothers and sister Marie had jobs that took them away for long hours.

In our home, most of the day, it was just my mother and me. I remember the summer, especially when I helped Mom do a lot of canning for our family.

The kitchen, in all its bright sunlight, held us captive for hours while I followed Mother's direction in helping her. We had a large, airy kitchen, and I can still see us working together in the many activities, and there was a sense of accomplishment.

The cherry trees were wonderful but not to me as much as Dad thought. His plan was that I would climb the trees and pick cherries since the boys were working. Me? I don't climb trees! But I did but not without complaining. A hard job as I remember. (Why couldn't they be big as an orange?) And then to make matters worse, I had to look at two more large trees filled with those little re cherries just waiting for me.

The backyard, before plump cherries appeared on the trees, was a delightful place. It was long and peaceful, and at the very back of the yard was a little sitting area with an arbor. Summertime changes when the cherries appeared. It was threatening to me and my peace. But I knew I had to at least try my best, and I can still see myself as I approached that ladder which wiggled with every step up I took. And my thought was, as I climbed, this is only one spot to pick—look at all the rest. Well, I talked myself out of looking at the big picture and did what I could. No one expected more than what I could do and seemed to appreciate my effort, and that gave me incentive to carry on. They seemed proud of me. How can I not try my best with this backing?

After picking each day, the following day I would help Mother pit the cherries and then help Mother can them. This was the best part, and I enjoyed pitting and canning with Mother. The "fruits" of our labor would be the wonderful, delicious cherry pies Mom would make.

All in all, I was most happy when the cherries were done for the season. Too many memories of hanging on to the ladder or the branch.

There were many times that Dad would remind me that "someday you are going to wish you had cherries for a pie from this wonderful tree." I always teased him back with "I doubt it." He would enjoy knowing that Rol's favorite pie is cherry, and that always reminds me of Dad and the summers of picking.

There was a summer that everyone could take a vacation from their war job, and we went to a cottage on a lake in Michigan. I can still see me as we drove closer to home, and I could catch a glimpse of the backyard and was so completely overjoyed when I saw the birds enjoying the cherries this year. Thank you, Dad! Did you plan it this way?

A JOURNEY WITH MY MEMORIES

The Cherry Pie Story

Some years ago, a lovely woman that went to the church we attended had a beautiful thing happen to her that has been a part of my joy ever since. God sees so many needs of the faithful, and it is a joy to be a part of something like what happened.

This woman—I have forgotten her name—so let's call her Mary.

Mary's husband ruled their household, and Mary was an obedient wife, except where it came to church.

He told her that she could not go to church nor take their children to Sunday school.

She said, "You can be in charge and make me do most anything, but you *cannot* take my church and my worshipping God away from me, nor can you take our children's time learning about Jesus away from them."

So he knew when he could no longer be in full control because he somehow sensed that this was something he could not do anything about.

Sometime later, she became ill. He had no idea of the love of church members for his wife and children and how members care about their sick. Night after night, a dinner was brought in, and he could not believe this and questioned "why?"

The reason I called this story "The Cherry Pie Story" is because that is what I took—and as it turned out, that happened to be his favorite pie, so I felt good about that.

Sometime, after she got better, she continued her practice of going into the darkened living room to kneel down at a chair to have her prayers before going to bed.

One night, she felt his presence beside her and looked up and saw him. Thinking he was going to say something that would be against God and prayer, she was hesitant and waiting.

However, the wonderful thing happened—he said to her, "May I kneel down and pray with you?"

God works through the love that we show. We must never forget that. Thank you, Lord.

I do not know any end to this story, but I want to think that it made a lasting change in that family and led him to the Lord. That has been my prayer.

George and Bob helped shape my life because I saw goodness in them. I wrote and read their eulogies at their memorial services because I wanted people who only knew them when they were older to know more about them. They were special, a gift, and I will never forget them.

FUNNY THINGS YOU REMEMBER . . .

My brothers used to say,
"How do you remember all those things?"

My Fun High School Years

The time to be in, after a date, was midnight. But going to a dance and then out with a group for hamburgers, that just didn't seem possible. There were other kids with dates there also, and we all came in at the same time, and then we had to wait. Always fun waiting, but you could not help look at the clock. My parents slept soundly, and I thought I was getting away with something by running to the clock that chimes on the dining room wall as fast as I could and bring the hands back to say 11:45 p.m.—my mother *never* questioned me in the morning as to how the clock was always fifteen minutes off, and I always thought I could get away with it. Ah, youth!

When climbing the steps to the second floor to my bedroom, I always had to skip over the third step because it squeaked, and while I was busy looking down and making sure I was doing it right, I was conscious of someone standing at the head of the stairs. It was my father with a lighted match in his hand. I said nothing for a moment because I was so surprised, but my father's only words were "just thought I would help you see your way up." Things like that are such sweet memories of how my parents handled things.

High school dances—most of the time, there was one on Friday and one on Saturday—it seems like that, but maybe it was almost every weekend on either Friday or Saturday, and they were usually at the women's club with a live band. We usually tripled dated, and that was special also. Have to say I didn't miss many—starting in my freshman year.

Love is what they gave us, and we never used it up

I need to say a few words personally about my brothers, George and Bob, and sister Marie. Our family unit made it because we were of one accord. We had love, we had faith, we had encouragement, we had loving support from our parents, and we all have enjoyed a life that matters. Our lives have been blessed with the mates we were married to: George and his sweet wife, Bonna; Bob and his dear wife, Dolores; Marie, with a strong companion in Arden; and me, with Rol who has blessed my life. And then our beautiful children and grandchildren. These are the treasures we find in living.

My brother George was strong for me all my life, and I went to him for that loving advice he always had. Not only for me but for anyone that asks. He loved life, he was gentle, he was a good businessman, and he knew his business and did well in it. He loved our family and his family so much. You cared, George, and I love you for it. You also gave me so many strengths. And we know where they came from. Thank you, dear brother.

My brother Bob—my sparring partner—only one year apart, and we probably took internal problems out on one another. Anyway, you too made me strong, dear Bob, by keeping me looking at myself and looking inside. We had some special times of grief together when Dad died, and I went up and found you in your bedroom, on the bed, crying. We both cried and helped one another. We all accepted that loss in different ways, Bob, and we were able to conquer the hard things and forgive the other things. Love is like that. Bob, I didn't know till your funeral what a giving and thoughtful man you were. I always knew how you cared about others but not in all those sweet and helpful ways you helped others that you met along the way. So many people came forth and said what you did to offer them help. What kindness, dear Bob. Thank you, dear brother.

And, Marie, you were a wonderful asset to our family. Talk about strengths, you had body strengths to help Mom in her need, and we younger ones would just look in awe in your love and protection. Marie, Mom and Dad must have loved you and loved your mother, my dad's sister, a lot to take you in as part of our family—a huge part. You made a big difference in the family and we all loved you in our times of growing up together.

Thinking back, that was a gift of love to you all your life, and I see that now. You and I had some "times" together because of you being six years older and me being the typical 'younger' sister. We found out later in life what we mean to one another, and I hope you felt that. I thank you with all my heart for all you did for our family. You were the glue at times that kept us strong when Dad was drinking. George and I expressed this one time, and we said that we owe a lot to you for being there for us. Thank you, dear Marie.

How much do we owe in life to a dear family? There is no price you can pay for it. I know there are families that do things right, and then some things don't work out as planned. You have to walk this walk daily to get this strength. You need to be in the Word, especially to get this strength, and you need others, not to tell you what to do but to just listen. May you find this in life.

Fun family times:

Another year has rolled around, and our father has announced, "Today is the day." The big circus has come to town!

These words bring such joy to us. Perhaps mainly because it was something my father loved to take us to, and we could feel his love for it, but also, it was such an exciting time of summer. The wonder of it builds as we prepare for the drive to the empty grounds, not too far but far enough. It was on the other side of town in Toledo where there were a lot of empty farm field. The fields were mowed down somewhat but still had high weeds in some areas. That was covered, then, with this sweet smelling sawdust, and it turned into something entirely different, something exciting to anticipate.

This was the day the trains were coming in and setting up, for the Barnum and Bailey Circus was arriving in town, and the public was invited to come and be a part of the magic of "Circus Day" as it had been experienced for over two hundred years.

We arrive full of excitement, and the elephants are already off the train—the tracks are right next to the large field where the circus will make its home while in town. The lovely sweet-smelling sawdust is down everywhere on the ground; the smaller venues are being set up and such interesting and colorful circus people walking around. Such a different life from what we were living.

But the big excitement, the big excitement is when the big tent is laid on the ground and ready to go up—this incredibly large piece of canvas— and the posts are laid out, and the elephants are at their stations. Soon, they will get their command. With a harness on them, they seem to inherently know their task and start at command to pull and pull and pull until this large tent starts going up and up, and then the special circus flags at the very top wave in the air.

We were allowed to walk all around—this, of course, is the day before the circus starts, and all the preparations are made, and it takes a lot of men to put it all together. We watch as the benches are put in the huge tent, and now it is time to imagine what it must be like to see the show for those who will have tickets for the amazing variety of acts in the "big top."

Many smaller tents were set up for the circus crowd that travel with the circus with such intoxicating names as "tallest person in the world," "fattest person in the world," "the man with tattoos all over his body," "the two attached women (Siamese)," "the bearded lady," "the snake charmer," the dwarfs (the little people), and many other fascinating people you could see if you paid to go in to see when the circus opened the next day.

There were clowns getting ready, lemonade stands being put up, cages put up where the lions are held until their trainer takes them into the big tent to perform.

It was still toward the end of the Great Depression, and we—a family of four children and our parents—did not have the extra money to attend the circus, but that never mattered. What mattered was what we were doing at that moment. The excitement of seeing the circus coming to town, being set up, and all the activity that goes with it. We were there each year, all day, and it was such a thrilling time. I can still see it in my mind's eye. We never were disappointed. This was such a family treat. Thank you, Dad, for having such a desire to show us this wonderful time, and we never even asked to "someday" go to the event inside. This somehow was enough.

At the end of this sunny day, we trudged back through the sawdust, out of the field to our car, and got in it for the ride home. Tired, happy, and still feeling the excitement

And now, as I go back in my remembrances of childhood, so many years later long after Dad and others in my family are gone, I go back to this place in my memory, and it remains a joy I shall never forget.

From the early morning hours, when the elephants pull the big top into the air to the very moment when the king pole races to the ground at the end of the day, you the public are invited to come and be a part of the magic of "Circus Day" as it has been experienced for over 200 years!

A NEW SONG TO SING
A New Home and Growing Up

It was 1940. It was at the end of the Depression, and those many affected were just getting their lives back in order.

It took a few years to complete this period because people were saving to buy a home again and regain some semblance of life that they left when the Depression hit them. This home we moved to was on the other side of town—we were always on the south side and now moving to west Toledo. In the transition, I don't remember leaving the one house for the other, but we were there, and that was all that mattered. We were happily running through our new home and neighborhood. This is where our family journey was now taking us, and it picks up where my real journey begins with such direction and zeal. We were all so excited.

This, to me, was a new song to sing because I was already feeling "liberated" emotions with growing-up feelings and heading to a new school and going into the sixth grade. There was no comparison to this feeling. I could sense that life would be different for me. I was growing up and more independent, continuing to love life, loving new friends, and recognizing some things in myself that were promising and exciting for the future.

They just were. And somehow, I knew that God was such a part of this. I knew because I felt direction.

I was always aware of what I wanted in my life, and my world had opened up to these wonderful possibilities ahead of me.

Our home was two stories with three bedrooms and a basement and an attic, a wonderful porch to sit on on a hot day and watching our neighborhood as it became known to us. Our home had a big airy kitchen and a breakfast room that my dad and brothers eventually added on with all windows that looked out to the yard and to the sour red cherry trees. The kitchen had a walk-in pantry which I approached cautiously since we found a couple of field mice enjoying their time in there in the winter. As you came in the side door, there was a landing, and you could go down to the basement or up to the kitchen. Along the side of the down side, I can still see our skates hanging up and other outdoor things with our heavier coats.

Life was beginning to pick up a pace that would go on till the war was over. They were hiring everywhere for war effort jobs which was called "defense work," and my father and then my brother George, after a while, worked at Rossford ordinance. My father was supervisor, and George was working at the PX (a military-base store) that was available to the Italian soldiers who were prisoners of war being held there. He liked getting to know them and learning their language. My sister, Marie, later joined them working there, and Bob got a job stocking at Bellman's market and worked weird hours. Long days for them, and it got to be Saturdays and Sundays also.

That left my mother and me alone in a quiet house in a quiet neighborhood. We kept busy. I helped Mom with the laundry (hanging up clothes on the clothesline) and canning, and Mom taught me a little bit of sewing on her old "white" sewing machine where years earlier, she made all our clothes, including our snow suits. It was a special time in our lives, I felt.

Mom was an "at home mom," and most things revolved around making a home for her family. My mom and dad still did not trust banks, and so Mom would go into town to all the utility companies to pay the monthly bills. That was a lot of walking all over town, but she did not complain because this was the decision they made until they felt comfortable, and funds were secured in the banks. They saved all these years so that my dad could go back into large construction building.

Our participation in the war would begin the next year after Pearl Harbor. No building was allowed during that time. I understand that my mother and father saved three out of four checks a month just with this in mind. We did not mind the sacrifice. We did it as a family. However, my father and mother always thought of the family first, and we had that special vacation to Niagara Falls as things got better and then bought our home. Mom got her first permanent in years, and things were changing.

We lived just a short distance from DeVilbiss High School where I would be going in a few years. At a couple of corners down the street, there were a few more stores: a drugstore with a soda fountain where kids hung out; across from that was Ernie's grocery store where we would be getting some of our groceries until the big serve-yourself markets came in after the war (like A&P). There was also Mom's bakery, and another block down was an ice cream store called "hi-spot" where my sister-in-law, Dolores, told me she first met Bob, my brother.

I remember, as we walked to school in the sixth grade, my new friends would come by each morning and call out "Ruth," and I would grab my books and run out to join them—that may just be an Ohio thing. Then we would walk to school together. You didn't go up to the door; you just called out. Seems funny now, but it was quite a system then. It worked! School was about five blocks away, and we came home for lunch.

My new school and sixth grade. Everything in my life changed. I felt independent and had many friends and especially liked boys and seemed to have a quiet interest in a new one each year. I always enjoyed school very much, and we had wonderful teachers that you would always remember because of their "unusual and unique personalities." Mrs. Pinardi who taught the music class and homeroom. She loved combining "O Sole Mio" with half of the class and "The Spanish Cavalier" with the other half, often! She also kept us in tune with things going on in the Metropolitan Opera and how it thrilled her when Patrice Munsel was made a soloist at the young age of eighteen.

Then there was Mrs. Goodyear that loved the boys in her class but not the girls and was quite a disciplinarian and was very strict in her teaching science. She made you move to the back of the row if you didn't know the answer to something she quizzed you on. Then sweet little Mrs. Hammond who had a little tuning whistle that she used, and we must have had more music there along with English.

And Mr. Skelton, who taught geography, was loved by all the kids. So many memories. And the friends. We loved sitting and sharing on the front steps of McKinley school. We had an outdoor dance at the end of school year and Mother made a new dress for me to wear. John McWilliam asked me to dance, and I remember it yet. (Inserting a newer memory, I joined John and his wife, Pat, and a group of friends in attending our sixtieth high school reunion together, and how good it was to see them all after so many years. Very special.) It was just an extraordinary time of growing up, and I loved every minute of it. Many friends over all these years.

Our country was in preparation for entering the war. On December 7, 1941, early on a Sunday morning, we all woke up to the incredible news that the Japanese attacked Pearl Harbor (Oahu, Hawaii). It shook everyone out of their apathy and encouraged a gigantic surge to help in all ways in the war effort. And men of all ages wanted to immediately join up—and women were also.

These were my growing-up years. *Radio shows like Jack Benny, Fibber McGee* and *Molly, and George Burns* went on weekly to encourage a nation at war and to bring a few laughs into homes that were sending their youth and husbands off to war. My father always lived with the thought that my brother George would go into the service. He remembered too much of his own time during WWI in France and was afraid for all George would have to go through, knowing it well. He was down on his knees, often, praying, and so we joined as a family during this time in solidarity with my father and his fear and my mother in her strength. George did go into the Navy in the Seebees Division and ended up, toward the end of the war, on Guam where there were Japanese soldiers hiding out in the caves in the rugged hillsides that didn't even know when the war ended, so they had to be careful—this from my brother George. (It was a great day when he came home and multiply that with all the other homes receiving their loved ones.)

I am skipping too far ahead. These were times of change and situations in the world that everyone was watching closely. The radio and news was on much of the time.

We attended the closest church because we lost our drivers while they were working. Mom wanted to attend the United Brethren Church (which was to like the Methodist—and then became united with them—she had always been in the Methodist church and so had my dad). My mother and I, and brothers—when they could—attended. Dad didn't. In those days, if you did anything that the church would call a sin (like my dad's occasional drinking), you felt strongly that you were not welcome. What a mistake the church made if this were true. Maybe it was only in my father's own mind, and he felt they would feel that way. Did they only minister to those who had no problems? One wonders.

My sorrow was that they did not have a good youth group, and what they did have was not what I needed. There was another Methodist church a short bus ride away that a lot of my friends from school went to, but I did not want to disappoint my mom by leaving the church where the family went. I think she would have understood though. I just didn't want to do that. I did the best I could to organize some activities in the youth group, but no one was interested. That was not much of a growing experience, but I grew in the Lord anyway. I knew it. I knew where I was going and to whom I belonged in the bigger picture.

Here I am at eighty-two, and I would not have changed one thing—not how my life was lived, not my family, not the knowledge of who I got my strength from, not my marriage with my dear husband Rol or children, Beth and Dave. I would not change a thing. I think I can safely say that I saw my life and followed its path. Living this life of mine has been full of exciting times and bright moments. I want to think that I sometimes made a difference in what I did. I have had, in my life, things to endure, but that gave me more strength for the road ahead. I don't think I was ever out of step with the Lord. I hope not. It was not intentional. I give Him all the glory in keeping me on a straight path and not having to meet that crossroads where a good and "not so good" choice had to be made.

In my early years, I thank my father that I saw what real pain was and in having a weakness that reared its head once in a while with his episodic period with the bottle. I thank the Lord for always protecting me, so I witnessed some of it but never was a part of it. I felt protected from it. It gave me a picture to carry all my life. But how I wish we didn't have it—but there you are. We did. I thank my mother for giving us this gift of strength in her Lord and knew He walked alongside her in all this pain she endured.

And I thank my husband that I got a chance to prove I can handle things also. There was never a time that I did not know and know for sure that the Lord was on this road with me, and the Holy Spirit was so strong, and I felt it.

So I will end here with much more in "growing-up times" in another memory to write. My years just kept getting better, and I became even surer of my direction.

This is where my Father's mother is buried in a Toledo
cemetery. And, above her casket is my parent's first child that
died within a few hours of birth - my sister.

WHEN THERE WAS THERE, AND THAT WAS THAT
Bits and Pieces

One is fortunate when life puts a glorious spell on it—loving times that make a difference.

We look to the past and remember that times were slower, and you had time to look at the particulars that you might miss. Like in present times that we are living in with all the electronics and people thinking so fast, when is there time to take in the glories of the Lord or just one another? It seemed that life and love had developed more slowly and with a forever meaning. Is life more transient today? One wonders.

Times of Remembrance:

The building is up, now the final paperwork and payment.

In the summer, I loved to go, once in a while, with my dad when he finished one of his buildings to the First Federal Bank of Toledo to do the final work on turning over the building to its owners and receive his final payment. It was always a good day of success. A couple of times as we were walking back to the car, we stopped to look into the window of a jewelry store, and Dad asked me if I needed a watch. Did I? I would love a new watch to replace my old Elgin. Well, he walked me into the store and let me pick out the watch of my choice. A surprise gift, and how I cherished it. Thanks, Dad.

Another time, I was in high school during these times; we walked past an office supply store, and I said, "Dad, we really need to replace our old typewriter if I am to help you type up some of your contracts and specifications and also help with my school work. What do you think?" He said, "Let's do it!" And we took home a beautiful new typewriter. That was special too. He was a dad that listens, understands, and makes decisions. I liked that about him. I especially loved these times together. I know he was proud of me and cared a lot for me. He was still introducing me to people when I was eighteen as his little girl. That embarrassed me, but how can you change the love of a father for you? I understood.

A Driver

One Sunday afternoon, I wanted to practice drive, and Dad took me out to Ottawa Park where there was a lot of room to drive. Bob and George also came along, but I was not sure this was a good thing. I did not slow down like I should on a curve. I ran over the curb and nearly drove up a tree. I heard many voices saying "slow down," and I did just in time. My dad just said, "You have to be conscious of curves and slowing down," but nothing so harsh that would scare me. I was scared and embarrassed enough.

It was a moment I did not want to recall and still shudder when I think of what I did and the awful chance I took with my family in being reckless. My father was unbelievably patient and understanding of this, and I never heard about it again, and I am sure he did not tell Mom. At least she felt, as usual, that what he said would be enough. I so liked that about her.

Newspapers

My brother Bob had a paper route and one of the down things about it was collection day. People seemed to love to get the paper but were not happy of being appreciative of the paperboy when he came to collect. He was almost, almost willing to forfeit the ones that gave him constant problems and just suffer the loss. I kind of felt sorry for him. We were close, only a year apart, and could feel his anguish but also could understand that he would like to make this extra money.

Several Sundays, when the paper was heavy and the weather totally cold with deep snow and ice, I decided to go with him on these quiet early Sunday mornings and help him as he pulled the sled with the heavy load of papers on it. He, in later years, thought nothing of cold weather because he would go out and sit on the ice in a chair and ice fish if he caught anything or not, so I should not have worried about him—but I did. I just felt he needed company. So we were out on the quiet streets and found it fun, and I know he appreciated it. It is hard for me to see anyone carry a heavy load all by themselves, and that has always been part of me. Plus, it was a fun thing to do, and it brings back many memories.

The Cottage

One year, at our family cottage at Vineyard Lake in Michigan, none of the other residents were there, and the dock had to be pulled in plus a couple of small boats, like the one belonging to my brothers. Bob and George went out in the cold winter wind, and I watched from the window. It was taking a long time, and they were having some problems with just the two of them handling this big task. I noticed their hands and ears and all. They were quite red, and the wind was relentless. I had a warm wool scarf that I went to get and ran out to the dock and put it around Bob's head and ears—George must have had some protection on—and that warmed me up too. My brothers were special to me. They are both gone now, but I will never forget them. They both were a strong influence in a quiet way in my life.

The Cottage—Special Times

Most weekends, we would go to the cottage on Vineyard Lake in Michigan. It is about one hour from Toledo, a nice drive through a lot of farmlands. The ride home was always great fun and relaxing, listening to the comedians such as Jack Benny, Fibber McGee and Molly, and Burns and Allen on Sunday evening radio.

Our time at the cottage was relaxed and fun. We would eat, eat, eat—play cards into the evening at a large dining room table. We would sit out on the swing in the front yard and look out to the lake and have great conversations. We took walks, frequently. We chatted with neighbors. We greeted visitors, played badminton, swam out to the raft, and greeted friends that we knew from high school. We shared in the dishwashing, cooking, and bed changing. On that trip to the raft, I usually talked one of my brothers to row me out there so my hair would stay wonderful—a typical girl thing. We have such wonderful memories of our time there.

My times there were cut short when I married and moved to California, but for many years after that, the family enjoyed their time there.

The Lakes around Toledo

Lake life and visits were frequent in growing up. Someone almost always would invite you if they have rented a cottage for a week or two.

Great fun. We were surrounded by many lakes: Clark's Lake, Devil's Lake, Vineyard Lake, and so many others. Many times there would be a dance at the lake, and that was fun to attend. The one at Devil's Lake had a roof over it, but the sides were all open to the lake. When I was dating in high school, I went to the lake quite often with friends, and we had a day or two with their families in the cottage. The lake life was one filled with many happy times, and how we enjoyed that.

Summers in Toledo

Relaxing and lovely—picnics, driving into the outlying countryside, being with friends, and dreaming time. We were surrounded with lakes, and it was so special visiting different ones.

The Quarry Called "Centennial"

A quarry for swimming is a large hole cut from rocks years ago and filled with water for a recreation area. I had many fun times there, and that bathing suit had to be just right because you were on view just as much as the guys were.

As it turned out, that was a favorite place that Rol took me to sit and hear the music from the dance area and kiss under that old moon.

Winters in Toledo

Slush, Dark, and Drab. Thank goodness for school and friends and dances almost every weekend with a live band, a happy time in life, football games, going "downtown" on the bus—everything was "downtown" before the little shopping malls came into being about 1939. Downtown was still the place to go to movies, shop, and work for some years, yet eventually, things were offered in neighborhood areas to accommodate needs.

Dreams of Leaving Toledo Someday

I was in high school, and it was during the winter months that I would say to myself, "You are not going to live here in this drab winter weather forever." I was sure of it—I did not know that meeting Rol would take me out of it. I thought I wanted to live somewhere where there were mountains in the background, and that is where we have lived—in Southern California. But since living in California and then returning to see my family in Ohio often, I do see so much more beauty and got acquainted with small towns that I did not know existed. So I claim my home state as a beautiful one, a great place to grow up and memories made.

Our First Home after Our Marriage

I was always living at home in Toledo, so I did not really know the costs of apartments, food, and just plain survival costs, so it was a genuine shock to me as we looked at apartments when we first arrived in California. The one we did rent was offered at $72.50, and I told Rol that I thought we should look further to see if that is right to pay that much. Seems funny now. That was cheap alongside of what it costs now. We went back and took that apartment. It was right on Huntington Drive (and Marengo) in South Pasadena, California. It had a large living room with a small dining area, a good-sized bedroom with bathroom next to it. The kitchen was light and airy and perfect for two people.

We had a door out to a small patio that we had breakfast on or even a light supper. Our laundry room was right out that door also, and we had a ritual of Monday night laundry that I would do, and Rol helped me a bit while he was also working on dinner. As I recall, it was usually something with hash brown potatoes and sometimes creamed chipped beef over toast. Did I ever get tired of that! Many times the washing machine was about to run out of the 25 cents per load, and Rol would tip over the machine to get the rest of the water out if that happened (to save another 25 cents)—you could go to the movies in Alhambra and see a double feature for 30 cents at a Edward's theater!

A Newlywed Shopper

Other crises occurred when I went to the market. I found a wonderful meat market in the middle of South Pasadena called Our Market. Hamburger—almost the best—costs 59 cents a pound. One day, we finished our marketing, and I said on the way home with our groceries, "Rol, we can't spend more than $15 a week on groceries on our budget." We had money in the savings, but that was designated for furniture and emergencies, and I didn't want us to go into that. So we had creamed chipped beef over toast—a lot! Somehow, you make it through by adjusting. All in all, on one salary for some time (another story begging to get to work myself to meet people and help with the budget), but you make it work.

Early Finances

Rol was a college graduate but was hired at a mere $225 a month, and we had to budget. But remembering back to those days, it was fun, and we both were involved and looked for inexpensive ways to live. Our car was paid for, courtesy of a wedding gift from Rol's parents, and our savings account looked good from a cash gift from my parents which my father started when he was still alive for each of us when we got married. Wasn't a lot but was big money to us then.

Rol took care of the finances for years, and it was not till we had our own travel business, and he had enough responsibility keeping tabs on those expenses that I asked to take over our personal finances, and that worked real well because I was very conscious of where the money was being spent. Rol worked with "envelopes that held money for utilities, etc." I, on the other hand, had an expense sheet I worked from.

Keeping the Courtship Alive

We always allowed money for our "courtship" dates. We loved going dancing at the Palladium often, and once a year, we would return to the Coconut Grove for dinner and dancing to celebrate our anniversary and remembrance of our engagement there in 1951. We loved the Mills Brothers, and Rol knew they were in town at a very small club in Los Angeles, and he made arrangements to take me there. What an evening. Our table was just about two back from them as they sang. I still remember that with joy. Anything Rol could do to bring happiness, he did. And I appreciated it so.

Rol bought a flower or some remembrance every Thursday for me because we were married on a Thursday, Thanksgiving Day. We had a blackboard up in our kitchen, and Rol always updated a dear message of how happy he was and love thoughts for me. That he did for years.

Just to show the cottage when we were young, and
Rol and I were visiting from California.

Scenes at Cottage

CHOICES THAT REFLECT CHRISTIAN VALUES

I wonder, when did I first notice God in my life? When did I notice Christ came alongside of me, bringing answers, illumining my soul? It was growing within me slowly. But it was always there, and I knew it.

I think I was waiting for something to come along to heal the wounds of my father. Someone had to do battle for my mother. I think it was my mother and her loving, quiet strength that helped bring peace to him.

You cannot win if you do not seek. My father was seeking control over drinking, memories over a lot of darkness of the soul he saw in his military role in World War I, his loss of his mother at the age of nine, his father getting remarried and having many stepsisters and brother, leaving his beloved father at an early age for the military. After marrying my mother one year later, after he came home from the war, he began to have his own family, even though it took a while, but his eagerness was always there.

Strange as it might seem, my father stopped going to church because of his drinking, and many others thought this way because this is the way the church looked at it in those days. That was sad because he loved the Lord, and you often saw him in prayer or asking me about my Sunday school lesson or having the family kneel in prayer together.

Their first baby died right after she was born, and that was not easy. Her name was Violet. Because my mother was hemorrhaging badly and nearly died herself, my father was sitting in the rocker in the room with her holding a perfectly formed baby who died at birth, and my dad held her in his arms and baptized her.

In 2006, my daughter and I visited the grave site where my father's mother was buried, and my sister, Violet, was buried in the same grave. As we sat and thought about it, I could almost feel my father's presence there as he stood at the grave to see his baby he loved lowered into the ground in that same grave site, where, at the age of nine, he saw his mother being buried there. I felt pain from my father and pain for my mother because she could not be there by his side as they participated in this time of loss. She had a time with her hemorrhaging, and they were working on saving her life. What a gift to realize that God both goes with this and goes before us in the person of Jesus in our suffering and difficult decisions. *"My Father, if this is possible, let this cup pass from me."*

Since it was 1930, and the Depression was in full swing, my father lost his construction business, and we were part of the Depression, even though he had much work with FDR's WPA program.

All that was part of my early life, but God was there. I knew it. I felt it through my mom and her beautiful face (quiet, steadfast faith) and the community of the church.

One thing I have learned is we all have our experiences in life. What we do with them is what counts. That has been my strength. I always knew there was joy in my heart, and I was a positive, happy person safe in God's love.

The yoke of the troubles in my family were sometimes heavy but at the same time light.

As is written in the Bible, Israel had deliverance from bondage from Egypt, and I related to the soft voice of God as he delivered us out of this sad time "in the valley." This is a bondage of my father's erratic drinking. To me, I would never be able to say he was an alcoholic, nor did I ever hear this said in our family. He just had an occasional drinking problem that was disruptive at times. All part of the journey. It didn't affect me because I was always forgiving of my father because of my love for him, and also, I felt such strong protection from him and from God.

What kept me strong as I grew was the unrelenting knowledge that God would not let us go and was always there to protect. He guided us, and I felt it. I knew it.

Right now, here I am at, writing these memories down—this was written when I was seventy-eight, sitting in the quiet beauty of the desert, remembering.

I know I am one of God's chosen. I have never doubted that. I have loved Him always as He has loved me. Somehow, he has always given the assurance of this.

Our son once said that he felt God had placed a blanket of protection over our family. How beautiful. How insightful.

I have felt this all my life—this blanket of protection, this strong desire to cling to Him, who can heal any wounds and give such strength. He has given me discernment, I know, and he not only whispers to me, he shouts to me of his love. I realize the immensity of God's love for me, and I give myself over to it. Growing spiritually has been my lifelong journey, and committing my life to him has been a natural consequence.

As it is written in Isaiah about the Son of Man, "surely he took up our infirmities and carried our sorrows . . . He was pierced for our transgressions. He was crushed for our inequities . . . the punishment that brought us peace was upon Him, and by his wounds, we are healed." *By his wounds we are healed.*

This is all part of our journey, and we each have a journey. I particularly love that thought, and it gives me peace.

I read the Psalms and think of all the pain our shepherd King David had. We should learn from the Bible that pain is part of it, and it's how we handle it is what is really important.

Now that I'm older, I can say that the Lord showed us how to accept all things in life, and what happens in early life is of endurance and sustains us in later life. Even "in the valley," there is so much greatness if you want it to be, if you look for it. God always shows me the way. You do not take it upon yourself; you cling to hope. I don't know any other way to live than that as a Christian, a follower of Jesus Christ.

Never have I felt that God ever deserted me. He gave me shafts of light and bright encouragement. These are gifts of grace from him.

We might think life brings us the impossible, but once we have been in the presence of His love, it never leaves you. Faith is a memory that is too beautiful and so attainable. God has shown me that I need to be in His Word. Faith like the good Shepherd, he wants me to know His voice and His will.

I love growth and living life like he has taught us in loving my enemies and being able to forgive, doing good to those in need, and being willing to share one another's burdens.

Trusting in God has been so much easier for me because God has come so near to me. I say this not in pride but in joy.

Choosing to celebrate in the midst of sorrow. It is a conscious decision, but it was possible because God was there to guide me even when my husband was so sick several times. Those were the moments that I surrendered totally to Him.

In living with the Lord and walking with him, we carve out a place in our hearts for others. Spiritually, it is about relationships.

In living with the Lord and walking with him, we carve out a place in our hearts for others. Spiritually, it is about relationships.

> My life has been a collection of things that has shaped my life in what I think matters whether it be inner calm, doing for others, or living a kingdom life. All of this makes life worthwhile and calls us to the life that is to come.
>
> Ruth Lampe, 10/20/10

This is what the Lord says:
"Stand at the crossroads and look;

Ask for the ancient paths,

Knowing Who You Are

Ask where the good way is,
And walk in it,
And you will find rest for your souls."

(Jeremiah 6:16—a favorite verse)

Memories of God's Direction
in My Life
and My Volunteer Work

We do not know where it leads, but it is enough to know that the Lord is with us and guides our path.

Thank you, Lord.

102

My life is an unfinished journey—how I choose to live it depends on me. Does my life have an expiration date? Yes, it does. May I have the courage to continue to keep on this journey of mine, looking always into the eyes of Jesus. Yes, I have.

My life has been centered on Jesus Christ. I have known this all my life. I knew the direction I wanted to go, and it was a journey with Christ. It also happened because my parents chose to raise me this way, and consequently, I chose to live this way.

I know for a fact that God loves me and that Jesus died for me. I am one of His chosen because He tells me this over and over again in the Bible. I know that God loves all of us equally—think of it, equally. I have done nothing to earn His grace, but I owe everything to Him. I thank God for protecting me, guiding me, answering prayers that are only good for me, and bringing so many wonderful and special people into my life to love and show His love.

Life is never easy for anyone because of the many ups and downs we face, and I have had these times, but the important thing is how I faced them, and what I do with them. And when I go to the Lord, He strengthens me.

I was asked once if my husband was a Christian before I married him, and I answered, "I would not have considered any other yoking, and of course, he was." It is wonderful to be able to grow together in Christ's love and guidance.

Our children have been a joy and easy to raise because they have always known about living for Christ and walking with Him. Both Beth and Dave come to us with prayer requests and we, them. Our son, Dave, calls when things are rough in his working world, and when he calls, he will say, "Mom, give me some verses that will help me through this," and we walk through the Bible together. I cannot tell you how many times we have been on the phone for a long time and just working through a problem with strength from the Word.

Many times, over the years, he would call and say, "Mom, are you and Dad home and available if I come over for prayer?" We always are. How many times were there when we knelt by the bedside and had long prayers to give us the hope and strength to go through a situation, and what a wonderful and exciting calmness we received from these times of prayer. Life is all about faith and obedience, and I think we have been blessed to see that and live that way.

My life has been confident that God cares about all my needs. I was an observer in life, the youngest in our family, and have memories of our life together. I guess I was a very normal child, but I knew what direction would be best for me, and I loved the assurances I got in growing up. It gave me preparation for my walk in life. I have loved life and people. What a blessing.

When I was at the University of Toledo, I was active in the "Y" program (and other groups) and accepted a leadership role but ended up being proposed to by my dear Rol, who was already a college graduate, so I made the big decision of getting married rather than going on. I was active in other ways there also. I did not go to the university the year after graduation because my father was diagnosed with only one year to live, and I wanted to keep that a special year with the family.

Married life and volunteering:

When we got married and moved on our honeymoon to California, we joined South Pasadena Methodist Church. They had an active Young Married Couple's Group, and before I knew it, I was corresponding secretary for the group! Then there was Circle, and after a few years, I was

Circle leader. Then there was Women's Society of Christian Service, and I was vice president. (These were child-bearing/rearing years, and I did this to keep active because neither one of us wanted me to work—it was more important to us to have me home with the children.)

When I was Circle leader, my circle was assigned to put on the yearly church choir banquet (small choir). I had two very small children, and no one in the circle could help for various reasons. That was not an easy thing, but I enjoyed it, and I did it.

I remember I had strawberry pies all over the kitchen, and then Rol and I drove to the church to put them in the refrigerator there. I made the meal and can't remember what it was. I had to go to the next WSCS board meeting, and they (the older, seasoned members) announced that the church choir dinner was put on by the Priscilla Circle, *but they made no money! I didn't know I was to make money also!* What a shocker. No, thanks for all the work that went into it, but thanks from the choir that "it was the best choir dinner they had had." Oh well, another hurdle and another lesson learned.

Then I was also active in community and social volunteering—vice president at the Junior Women's Club in South Pasadena the year I was pregnant with David then. I had volunteered once to work on the Sister Kenny Foundation Drive in our city, and that takes a lot of time getting volunteers. This was when polio was still a threat and being treated at a city close to Pasadena, Duarte.

One year, they could not get anyone to head it up and called me. I said, "No, I am sorry, but I just could not." They said, "Someone else will take the lead!" and I finally said that I would help her but not lead. Little did I know that this woman was a member of a prominent social organization in the city and *had* to "serve," and they put her on this—she was new in town and did not know a single person. So guess who had to do all the work to get volunteers? My uncle in Pasadena called me the day after I said I would "help only," and then he said, "Look in the *Star News* in the front section about page 5, in big print, above the fold!"

"Mrs. Roland P. Lampe accepts chairmanship of the Sister Kenny Drive for South Pasadena." *I did not!* But what could I do? I did it and very rarely ever heard from that "presumed chairman" because she did not participate. *Lessons learned!*

When we moved to Costa Mesa, California, we were looking to join the local Methodist church. To show you how much they needed my husband Rol and me, here is the story: we visited the local Methodist churches, and I have to share with you a couple of funny things that happened while we visited several times.

I was a guest at a Circle meeting in this very sweet, small house that was in the older part of Costa Mesa. During the meeting, the hostess, a very nice lady whose house we were at, was up on a stepping stool getting down from the top shelf dishes she was going to use to serve dessert on and participating in the meeting as well, by talking and responding. Her kitchen area was right next to her small living room, and as she took each plate down, she *dusted* them off. I was not used to someone not being prepared, and it still brings a smile to my face. That was one thing.

The next happened the day after we first visited the church. It was a hot, sticky July Monday. We were living in an apartment for six weeks while they finished the home we bought. We had to move quickly because the new buyers of our South Pasadena home had cash to pay for the home, and we left within a week of escrow, probably two weeks in all, and our friends from South Pasadena said, "Boy, when you make a decision, you really move."

Our dear pastor, George R., came to visit the night before we moved, sad that Rol, one of his supporters, would not be there any longer. The church was pretty divided in a church problem to stay where they were or to move to another location, and many did not want to move. Rol just supported—we loved that sweet, old church sanctuary, and over the years, it proved that the move was not a good idea. It was on a hill and not one you could walk to like the other. It was so nice of him to call, and we couldn't help feeling like we were deserting him.

On with my Costa Mesa church story. Well, those were the days when it was hot, and you were young; you wore this little cloth, this elastic thing as a top. I was out with the children and saw this man in a dark suit and pretty serious looking, walking toward me—*the same man I saw in the pulpit the day before.* I said, "You look familiar—didn't I just see you yesterday in the pulpit?" The answer was yes. I asked him in. What else could I do?

Our little daughter Beth was almost five and going into kindergarten in September, and our son, barely two years old. And guess what the two-year-old wanted to do? He wanted to climb all over me because of this stranger being there and consequently kept pulling on my little elastic top that I was afraid would shock that superstaid pastor for a lifetime. I did not know how to get up without drawing attention to what I needed to do and change to a bra and blouse, so I sat there, and he wanted to chat far longer than I wanted to. End of that church, for a lot of reasons.

Next try: we went down to visit a beach church. Should have gotten the clue that they needed leaders when we saw one name—*one name only*—Bill McDonald, as chairman of the trustees, chairman of the Pastoral Relations Committee, lay leader, and chairman of the official board! *Help!*

There was no other choice, and we liked the young, unorthodox pastor. Why the bishop put him there makes one wonder; he unnerved those—mostly old—people no end by his unconventional ways. He was a former "rough type" merchant marine who used to boast of leading services on shipboard because he was the token preacher's kid and should know something in order to preach on Sunday on the ship. He also had a young wife who loved to startle the old women of the church because she wore some wild outfits, and when they complained, she only dressed with more conviction.

Within eight months of joining this church, Rol was superintendent of the Sunday school, and I was president of the Women's Society. We did that for several years and went home every Sunday after church, wondering "what just happened!"

At my meetings, there was the same little lady, Miss Newland, that followed Rol around and complained all the time to the pastor because Rol used the Sunday school money to buy crayons and cutting shears that were needed for the children. (Offering went through the church first, and he put in a requisition to be reimbursed.) And to me, she would put this little bell to ring—to keep order presumably—on the desk where I presided, and I saw it but refused to use it, but that did not stop her. She put it there each meeting.

Our discussions were mostly about silverware that was missing from the kitchen, *and "it must be the junior high kids that took it, and they should not be allowed in the kitchen." Incredibly enlightening and enriching stuff.* They had an official board where several people opposed everything, and those meetings were an attack on our poor pastor for the most part, but he took it well! He was our friend and was there for us many times. This was material that only Hollywood could write, and we were in the midst of it.

One night, when we were already in bed, and I thought Rol was asleep, I opened my eyes to see him leaning over me and saying, "Did you ever think the superintendent of Sunday school would be in bed with the Women's Society president?"

That really made us laugh. There were many Sundays where he had to lead a lot of classes because so many teachers called late Saturday saying they could not be there to teach. Incidentally, our daughter, Beth, loved those times because she was so proud of her daddy, and it was so special to her being in that large group he had to gather together to do all the teaching.

In the meantime, Dave was in the nursery, and the lady they hired to sit gave out sugar cubes to keep the children happy!

We were members for a few years and then left because by that time, they opened a new church closer to our home, and our children would be where some of their school friends were.

Things didn't get much better because that church had some "built in" problems that were unbelievable.

During the time we were at that church, I was asked to be District Secretary of Spiritual Life for the Women's Society (conference level) and did that for four years and then was asked to be District President of the Women's Society. This entails being helpful to the WSCS of fifty-two Methodist churches in the Whittier District, which included our area. That was interesting, and I loved giving spiritual life messages and workshops during that time, but then again, it was one meeting after another, plus every year, you serve; you are put on several other boards and committees like Camp Commission and Retirement Homes, invited to the yearly Board Meeting of the Arcadia Methodist Hospital which the Women's Society owned and gave their report to. When I finished, I was worn out, and my family was tired of it. I was on forty-two boards and agencies at the end of these eight years, and then I felt like I was being groomed to be conference president. *No way!* I just would not be able to continue to give that time. And I never regretted it.

By this time, our children were entering junior high—Beth was anyway—and we felt an urgency to find a church with a good youth group, and we did. The battles with our church were continuous with little spiritual guidance and growth that we needed.

I called our district superintendent one Monday evening and said, "Bill, we are thinking of leaving the Methodist Church because we do not want to lose our children to the church and their relationship with God, and we are getting nothing that inspires us." I then commented to Bill, "There are so many churches in the area that were doing such great things in the youth department." Bill said, "I want to tell you something, Ruth— go where it is at! I am telling you this as a friend."

We visited churches and chose St. Andrew's Presbyterian to be our church home. It has been a spiritual walk with the Lord which we greatly needed.

After being so busy in volunteer work, it was a delight to just sit and "be fed."

Our children went to the wonderful church youth group led by Kim S., and it was a large group. They went to work camps with the youth.

We have been members for about forty-one years and have served with joy where asked. However, at the first, it was a time of refreshing myself in the Lord and renewal.

Rol was active and then became president of the Men's Fellowship early on—then he was active in working with Reverend Paul S. setting up the Covenant Group Program. He was on session and became clerk of session. He was active on the mission committee which is a first love of his. He had been a Sunday school teacher for a lot of years at all the churches we have belonged to and loved that best of all and served on the Vacation Bible School team often.

Then, I served as a Stephen minister for some years, a deacon with Rol, vacation Bible school teacher, and this past year, the prayer leader which was a highlight in so many ways for me. I love those little children and telling them about Jesus and how to talk to Him in prayer. It was a blessing. Rol and I have both gone on missions (Rol Mendenhall, Miss and me Romania).

I had been a Bible leader at Heritage House which is very challenging, working with these women who are living there because of some real problems and a life all mixed up. It was a bit hard for me, but I wanted to do it. When I questioned God about my being relevant to these girls coming from my different backgrounds (keeping out of trouble I guess is what I am saying), God just asked that "I tell them about Him, and He would do the rest."

That relationship with Heritage House stays with me, and I so loved sharing about Jesus and seeing changes in many as we participated in the Bible study. Such a worthwhile mission.

I had been "scribe" for about nine years for our C. S. Lewis Study Group and sent out a lot of messages and reminders. We studied and learned. I may be forgetting something, but best of all, I have loved leading the "Memory Writing Class." It has been exciting, fulfilling, and fruitful. I had been in many prayer groups and specific prayer groups and intercessory prayer through Lydia. I served with Lydia on a Lenten "Day of Prayer," and Rol and I, plus some volunteers which we could not have done without, like Betsy and Nancy, and we put together five hundred journals for prayer and also bookmarks that were pictures of families from the church praying—and their testimony regarding prayer in their family life. I was asked to put together a mission/prayer journal for the children's department, and that was very special working with Trevecca on that.

And I do not think the Lord is finished with me yet. I hope not. I recorded some of my activities, so I had a remembrance of ways I served. In all of my mentioning, what I did reminds me of the joy I found in serving.

Note: This was intended to be a private record for me until I wrote the book on *memories* and found that this was a big, active part of my life. All this is only my record of what I want to remember with joy in serving.

Lenten prayer bookmarks and journal; *a God thing*—sending Jane Bernard to Mendenhall, Mississippi; *our family prayer journal*—created the booklet, and David A. did the final graphics, and it was given to each child in the children's ministry; Church Lenten readings, 2007; Heritage House experiences and booklet I helped create ways and made copies of Bible verses given to the girls of Heritage House during Bible study the day I had the Bible lesson. They loved these handouts; church mission trip to Romania in 2004. Our daughter, Beth, and granddaughter, Stephanie, went also. I was so pleased about that; a week in San Francisco at Glide Memorial Church—learning about the hippie generation (through the Methodist church); prayer leader at vacation Bible school at Saint Andrews 2009; teaching "conversational English" to foreign neighbors (Korean); a week at Oxford; and a week at Cambridge at the C. S. Lewis Oxbridge seminar.

OUR FAMILY AND MY LIFE:
An Over-All Look
Ruth Carolyn Kuehnl Lampe

Some of my stories may be repeated but this recap shows the timeline of a lot of things during the years. Many of my stories were written during my time at attending or leading the Memory Writing Class at church and they may overlap. Sorry about that. Ruth

My mother and father were married on Thursday, June 24, 1920, the following year after Dad returned from serving in WWI (France) in 1919. They married in 1920.

They had a home across from the family grocery store on City Park Avenue, Toledo, Ohio, and my father started his own building construction business which grew to a large construction business because of his workmanship and his talent for it and his integrity of being honest. (The records from his family in Vienna said that building and architecture was a major occupation of family members.) Note: I always thought my grandfather came from Vienna, but my cousin Marcia's research—through her visits to family members there and also correspondence—indicates that our grandfather was not from Vienna but from Teplitz, Bohemia.

Grandpa Kuehnl had a brother Wendelin, however, who migrated/ moved to Vienna and established a construction company which, she was told, so impressed Grandpa Kuehnl that he encouraged his son, George (my father), to follow suit. Grandpa Kuehnl bought up lots across from the store on City Park Avenue, and after my dad learned the construction business (from Uncle Fred Haas's family), he had my dad build houses on those lots. Possibly, the starting point of his in the construction business.

Bohemia was an area populated primarily by Germans and located in what is now the Czech Republic. It was a self-sustaining kingdom but was incorporated/gobbled up into the Austro-Hungarian Empire, never to exist independently again (according to the information from Cousin Marcia and her research). In fact, Prague (Prag) was originally a Germanic city in this Bohemia. She said, "I believe Hitler went after that area when he attempted to reunite the German Volk once again. At least that was the reason he gave for entering Czechoslovakia."

The war was over by this time, and Dad was able to build our home at 2028 Marlowe Road. We moved in November 1946. (I went to the Libby/DeVilbiss football game by bus with girlfriends and froze—it was so cold—came home, and sat in a hot tub to thaw. I was a junior in high school; no building was done during those war years.)

Their first child, my sister Violet, was born and died the same day in 1921. She was delivered at home, and the doctor left before he fully cared for my mother who was hemorrhaging, almost to death or the baby. My father sat in the rocker across from his very ill wife with the tiny new daughter in his arms, already dead, and he baptized her. She was perfectly formed. (They never had another child born at home after that experience.) She is buried in Forest Cemetery, Toledo, Ohio. My father had her buried in the top part of his own mother's grave, and when I visited there with my own daughter, Beth, in 2006, I could *feel* my father's presence, with my mother too ill to be there, grieving for their dear dead child and memories of his own mother dying when he was nine. I noticed that Violet's name and dates were not on the Rosewood grave marker, so I had arrangements made to have the marker inscribed, below our grandmother's name: Baby Violet, born and died 1921. It made me pleased to be a part of this.

Then they had a stillborn child (I believe, a son) and grieved another loss. It was mentioned in the family Bible, but Mother didn't talk about things like that in those days, so I never heard it from her.

Because of my father's sister Bertha's death, they raised her child, Marie, because there were other children, and she asked they do this. They did and loved her so much. She really was an important part of our family and always one of the family.

My father's business prospered, and they built a home on 3534 Glynn Court in the South end of Toledo where we were all brought home after our births at Flower hospital.

Their first living son, my wonderful brother George Edward Kuehnl Jr., was born October 3, 1927, and that must have been a joyful time.

Just at the time that the Great Depression was looming, their second son, Robert Joseph, another special brother, was born on January 15, 1929.

Then me! A little girl by the name of Ruth Carolyn was born January on 14, 1930.

Even though the Depression was hitting most everyone hard, especially in the building trades, my mother and father were able to, by my estimation according to the school grade I was in, keep their home on Glynn Court until 1935-36. FDR came into office in 1932, and this might have been 1934 to 1935. (I can tell by the grade I was in—Mother sent me to Harvard School Kindergarten with my brother Bob, and they said I could go to kindergarten with him, but I must stay two years—both born in January, probably was accepted because of January birthday and because of the long walk to take us and pick us up again. I loved those walks each day but didn't think that my mother had to walk it four times with Bootsy, our dog, by her side. In school, I loved Billy Goat Gruff, so it seemed to suit me.)

I either finished the last part of my second year of kindergarten at Harvard or at Arlington School when we moved to Shasta Drive. The business was gone, and the money tied up in unfinished buildings that could not go forward and in the banks giving out just a bit at a time.

Sometime during this period of time, my father started working on the Erie Canal to get it ready to become the Anthony Wayne Trail. Mother said (we have pictures of this) that he had one thousand men under him as he served on the WPA (Work's Project Administration under the New Deal when Franklin Delano Roosevelt was President). I do not know but presume, from the times involved, that he worked on that the latter part of our time on Glynn Court. I am not sure of this. (Not sure on timing here.)

We lived on Shasta Drive for a short period (less than a year) during the middle of my first year in first grade at Arlington (I believe). My father, who was always such a good provider, was unemployed and started drinking heavily. (I do not know where he was working at that time, and it might have been between WPA jobs, but I do know he was not at home during the daytime.) It was a desperate time for our family, but with the wonderful, beautiful, steady faith of my mother, we pulled through but not without many adjustments to living and surviving during the pain of seeing my father in his out-of-control drinking. I loved school and the teachers and being "big" like Marie and George and Bob and going a full day to school!

Sometime in 1936, all but my father went to live with my Grandpa Klotz (my mother's father) and her sister, Aunt Esther, for eight hard months. Hard for many reasons, but the big reason is that my father started working for WPA about that time, and he was out of town or wherever the work was assigned to him as superintendent of projects, and there was no room for him at Grandpa's home. So he lived in downtown Toledo in a small hotel. (I think it was called Willard.) He was terribly missed and would come on Sundays by bus to see us, and we would watch for him to come down the street. What a joy.

After the eight months at Grandpa's home on Lodge Avenue in Toledo, my mother and father rented a home at 952 Western Avenue, not far from Grandpa's home. We then started Walbridge School. For the most part, my father and mother were able to start rebuilding because my father was working steadily with the WPA.

History of President Roosevelt's New Deal—the use of this information was provided by resource from the Ohio History Central World War II—

"The New Deal was a major component of President Franklin Roosevelt's plan to help the United States recover from the Great Depression.

"In the presidential election of 1932, Franklin Delano Roosevelt . . . Roosevelt declared that he had a plan to assist the American people. Known as the **New Deal**, Roosevelt's plan proposed utilizing federal resources in an unprecedented manner to aid the American people. Roosevelt hoped that his **New Deal** would allow Americans to cope with the Great Depression, would help end the current economic downturn, and would help prevent another depression from occurring in the future. Because of his **New Deal** proposals, Roosevelt handily won the election.

"As president, Roosevelt immediately set about implementing his plan. Upon assuming office in March 1933, Roosevelt provided guidance and leadership that many Americans desired. Because of the severe economic crisis, most bills that the president proposed received Congress's immediate approval. Roosevelt first hoped to alleviate the suffering of the American people and to implement programs that would help meet his citizens' basic needs. One of his first moves was to declare a bank holiday so that the federal government could help struggling banks to become solvent. Roosevelt proceeded to create additional government programs and offices that provided aid and jobs for the American people. The Federal Emergency Relief Administration, the Civil Works Administration, the Public Works Administration, the Agricultural Adjustment Act, the National Industrial Recovery Act, and the Civilian Conservation Corps all provided relief to the American people, including government jobs. Roosevelt and the Congress implemented these various programs and agencies between 1933 and 1935, and they became known as Roosevelt's First New Deal."

"Unfortunately for the United States and its citizens, these various government programs failed to provide relief to all needy Americans."

A second New Deal was implemented:

"The Second New Deal focused more on ending the current depression and implementing safeguards to prevent another depression from occurring again. There were still programs designed to assist the American people, including programs like the Works Progress Administration and the National Youth Administration, by hiring people, especially men, for government positions."

"Both Roosevelt's First New Deal and his Second New Deal assisted the American people, including Ohioans. Hundreds of thousands of Ohioans received government aid through one or more of these programs or agencies. Unfortunately for the American people, all of Roosevelt's efforts came to naught. They did not end the Great Depression. At the same time, it is important to remember that Roosevelt's efforts did alleviate some

Americans' suffering. The event that finally ended the Great Depression in the United States was World War II. This conflict provided millions of Americans of both genders new jobs and opportunities as the nation mobilized for war."

I have added this information about what transpired in the nation to allow some turn-around which affected our family immensely.

We had much peace again with our family all together. Dad was gone most Mondays through Fridays, and it was so special when he came home on Friday night but then had to leave again on Sunday. It enabled us to build quiet strengths again in our home life.

My mother kept a "home," and we felt secured and loved. She was a wonderful cook, and she cooked marvelous meals and kept our home spic and span. (It seems that when we came home from school, the rugs were always wet from her scrubbing them, but I am sure that wasn't true.)

My father had some episodes of drinking, and they could be traumatic, but we made it through. My mother was so strong, and I only saw her cry once in my life, well, maybe twice when I did not tell her I was going to a friend's home to play on the way home from school and—I was in about the fourth grade—and I walked in the front door, and Mom was standing, and Marie, George, and Bob were sitting, and I could feel the tenseness because they did not know where I was or what could have happened to me. Never happened again.

My mother never once scolded me. I could always depend on her to say, if something happened, "What part did you play to make it happen?" Got me every time—never took sides but treated us all fairly and evenly. I believe we all lived our lives to show her our love, but I will say more about this special mom in my story about her.

In the summer of 1937, we were in the school district of Walbridge School and started there, and I think I was in the second or third grade. We moved to 952 Western Avenue (rented home) in the south end of Toledo, not far from Grandpa's home. Dad and Mom took us all on a wonderful family trip—so like him to think of family first after the trying one and a half years we had and with the first monies he was now earning with the WPA and things picking up again, economically. (I have attached a picture of cabins we stayed in on our trip to Niagara Falls, and I love that Mom put on the back cabins we stayed in on our trip to Niagara Falls, 1937.)

Great Family Fun: a driving trip to Niagara Falls, a special and wonderful time. We went on a family trip that was just wonderful. We all piled into the family car, and Dad drove us to Niagara Falls (hard to believe that it is only two hundred miles from Detroit, but with the roads and the slower cars, it seemed like we had a wonderful, probably a week, away). We stayed in these darling little cottages along the way, and I think we traveled all the way East on Highway 240, and it was pure joy.

It doesn't take much to see how much my father loved his family.

We lived on Western Avenue from 1937 till summer of 1940. We moved to the west end of Toledo, and my parents bought their first home since the Depression hit, and we had to leave the Glynn Court home—on Upton Avenue. We kids were so excited and explored the whole neighborhood. We lived there during my sixth grade (McKinley School) to junior year in DeVilbiss High School in 1947. The war was over; construction could begin again, and my dad and Mother had saved all those years so he could start in his construction business again, and one of the first things he did was build us a new home on Marlowe Road, 2028 (both of these houses close to DeVilbiss High School where we went to school).

Life was especially good for me when we moved, and I started sixth grade at McKinley and then on the DeVilbiss. I was growing up and the real, real me was developing, and it was so special to me.

My father worked long hours and lots of times seven days a week. My parents had been saving all their checks all these years since his WPA jobs started, and they lived, as I recall, on one check and saved the rest (*not* in a bank, in case those could go under again but under the Wardrobe in a strong box). Their hope was that he would be able to start up his business again in construction, but this could not happen till the War (WWII) was over.

In 1939, the war in Europe was suffering, and they needed our help, but we did not enter it until United States and Great Britain declared war on Japan on December 8, 1941. (I was eleven.)

The Japanese attack Pearl Harbor on December 7, 1941, and on December 11, 1941, Germany declares war on the United States.

Everything changed, and we were fully in the war effort. My mother and father had the news on often, and things in the world were dreadful, especially in the year of 1939 when Hitler marched into Poland and all the desperate things done to the Jews and others in Europe.

I graduated from high school in June 1948. Wonderful years for me.

It was a hard time for my parents when George was serving in the Navy but then so many families were anxious also. It was pure joy when he returned home on the General Mann troop ship.

On April 18, 1945, German forces in the Ruhr surrender.

On August 14, 1945, Japanese agree to unconditional surrender.

My dad goes back into his own construction business.

He builds a new home for us on 2028 Marlowe Rd (in my junior year in high school).

My brother's joined him in the business and proceeded to carry it on after his death and to great heights, and he would have been so proud. He just knew they could do it.

My father's health began failing and was told by his cardiologist in late 1948 that he probably only had a year to live. He had to stop smoking and drinking and had take it easy.

We had the most wonderful family year of my life. He was home a lot, and we had wonderful family times of just being together. His last breath always was in thinking of us. I will always remember that year. I think my mother must have been the happiest of all to have him back again fully to her.

My father died in Toledo hospital on December 7, 1949. He waited till my mother got there and just held out his hand for hers in saying his goodbye.

Thank you, Dad!

Always a dad, thinking of us. Shortly after my father died, my mother had a dream, and in it, my father told her that he wanted to have her buy a cottage "to keep the family together."

That next day, in the paper, she saw a cottage, fully furnished, for sale at Vineyard Lake in Michigan, about an hour away. She called the realtor, and we drove there that day—Mom, Bob, me, and the realtor. It was so precious and too good to be true. Mom bought it right away, and the family had many wonderful years there. God works in such special, special ways. Thank you again, Dad.

I forgot to say that church has always been a very important of my life. My parents were strong Christians and saw to it that we always went to church. I have always had Jesus in my life and have known it so strongly. He was leading me and guiding me and protecting me. More later about my walk with Him.

I graduated from DeVilbiss High School in June 1948. Curious that in the back of the year book, where they give your accomplishments and have a quote to summarize you, it said, "Wins us all." (That was interesting to me because I had friends in all social groups and otherwise and loved them all. They meant a lot to me—is that what they mean? Whatever, I thank them for this kind thought.)

When my dear father died on December 7, 1949, I was nineteen. We had a wonderful last year of his life because he was not allowed to drink or smoke, and his cardiologist said, "What time you have left will be a gift" because his health/heart was so bad. His death was and has always been one of the big losses in my life. His little girl was left without his strength. He gave me more than a gift of life.

My college was delayed a year because I wanted to spend as much time as I could with family, so I started at the University of Toledo a year later and was enjoying it so much and was getting involved in other activities at the university, but on July 1, 1950, my husband, dear Rol, came into my life, and we married November 22, 1951.

Marriage: November 22, 1951

Beth Ann born: October 5, 1954

David Paul born: June 8, 1957

See additional reports for my life.

Timeline: Ruth, Born 1930

Lived at Glynn Court till 1935 or 1936

Lived at Shasta Drive, Lodge Avenue, and then Western Avenue, 1936-1937

Moved to Upton Avenue (sixth grade), Summer 1940

Moved to Marlowe Road in 1943 (Junior Year in High School)

Bonna and George got married in January 1949

My father died in December 1949

Bob and Dolores got married in July 1951

Rol and I married and moved to Southern California in November 1951

Mother died at the age of ninety-four in a home in Waterville, Ohio, in 1987

Brother Bob died on March 21, 2007

Brother George died on November 11, 2008

Compiled by Ruth Kuehnl Lampe, October 2008, and dedicated to my mother and father

(There are things in life we cannot explain, but all in all, if love is there, life becomes more precious.)

MY MOTHER'S FAMILY— THE KLOTZ FAMILY

My mother was raised in a church going family. She said Sunday was devoted to church all morning and again in the evening. Saturdays, she said, they spent preparing tasty food to eat on Sunday and always had a big Sunday afternoon dinner after church. Mother said that the day was filled with friends over, and it was so special.

Now back to my mother's family:

1. William John. Born 1891. Died 1994. One hundred four years old and no dementia. Maybe it was the four women he married that kept his mind active. He married young, and they had a son, Ben, and she died soon after, and I do not have that history. He and others helped raise Ben till he married Aunt Louise. She was a schoolteacher. I don't know much about his work experiences, but I do know my dad got him a job as a sales person at a lumber company.

They had a daughter by the name of Janette. As I understand it, Aunt Louise and he belonged to a married couple's group at their church. After Aunt Louise died, one of the widows of the group started writing him and then marriage. Each time a wife of his died, another widow in the group wrote him, and they became pen pals and then married. This happened two or three more times with widows in that I was told.

2. Bertha Elsa Klotz Kuehnl (my mother). She was born on March 21, 1894, and she died on January 2, 1987. She had Alzheimer's for years. She was almost ninety-four. (More about her under "Mother")

3. Martha Klotz (Aunt Marsie). Died before my mother, but I don't have the date. She was such a special, sweet auntie. Her father, having five daughters, had to marry them off, and it didn't work with my mother, but he chose Will Liebelt for Aunt Marsie, and she deserved so much better than that. I wonder if she was happy. I believe she was because she made the best out of every situation. I loved her for that. Uncle Will bought and sold farms. He was not a farmer. Aunt Marsie loved animals and loved having them as her friends. She named them all. They came to her when called but not to him. (The sheep know the shepherd's voice!) He would have aunt Marsie fix up the farms and make them very pretty and homey, and they would sell them at a profit.

My father used to say that when he took his coin purse out of his pocket and opened it up, moths flew out of it. He had an industrial accident when he was working for, I think, Willys-Overland (Jeep), and something flew off a machine, and it cut into his mouth. From then on, he had no teeth because he had no proper gums for them to hold the teeth. They eventually moved into the city and lived on Manhattan Boulevard, not too far from Flower Hospital.

I hesitated having Rol meet these relatives because you don't bring out all your relatives when you meet the man you want to marry, and Uncle Will and his family were a bit different. We finally visited them on a visit with our children to Toledo, and it was at a time that our son, Dave, was feeling a little punk because Beth, his sister, was having teeth come out, and the good fairy brought a gift of money—when Dave and his incredible, busy mind looked up at Uncle Will and his teeny little mother who had two pair of reading glasses on, both of them without teeth, I just knew what was going through his mind and prayed he would not mention anything like "wow, the good fairy must have been good to you!" We made it through but talked and laughed about it after.

Aunt Marsie did not have a, what you would call, an exciting life being married to Uncle Will, but he was a good provider, and when he died, she was left with enough to live comfortably, and it pleased me, in the end, when she had Alzheimer's, that she was put in a lovely convalescent home, had her hair done, finger nails done, and looked fantastic. I was at last pleased for her and her sweetness as she was surrounded by people that looked after her so well because she was such a dear.

She told me once, when we were talking about neighbors, that she never had a neighbor she did not like. That said volumes to me, and I have always remembered that. In order to have good neighbors, you have to be one!

4. Lydia Klotz. Died on February 4, 1987, at ninety-two, one month after my mother. After her own mother died suddenly, Aunt Lydia wanted to go away to school to become a nurse, in the worst way,

but her father did not believe women should be nurses. It wasn't a proper occupation, he said to her, but she finally convinced him to allow her to go to the Missionary Alliance College in Newark, New Jersey. She was training to be a missionary for Africa and then had some kind of heart situation or illness that they thought weakened her heart, and the school said no to that, so she became a social worker in Harlem, living by the school and going by underground, to do her social work. And I think that would have been a most interesting period of her life.

I will have to look at the oodles of journals she wrote in to see what just happened, if she has it documented. As time went along and she remained unmarried, she started taking care of her pastor's wife and became very acquainted with his family. Sometime after Lois, the wife of Uncle Herman, died, he asked Aunt Lydia to marry him. I was saddened when she told me that she had to buy her own engagement ring—a sweet, very tiny diamond—because she did not make much money, and he made very little in his congregation. He had a church for a while. His kids were grown and all married people. She wore that sweet little diamond ring until she died, and it was given to one of Uncle Herman's granddaughters after her death.

Gradually, he took a church in Muskegon, Michigan, and we visited them a few times there on the way to Rose Lake near Cadillac, as I recall. After that, he had heart problems, and they were not assigned another church—I do not believe—and took an assignment in operating a summer camp for boys and girls somewhere in Ohio/Michigan area. I understand Aunt Lydia loved working with the kids.

After that, he could not work, and providence stepped in, and relatives from California wrote to other relatives to see if there would be anyone willing to come to California to care for a cousin, Melissa Repine, because she was found by other relatives that she was mistreated terribly in a convalescent home—very senile—and they wanted to have someone in the family come and sign her out, and they would get the lawyers to get her money back that she signed over to them. That was before the State of California had a law that they could not do that. They wanted someone to come and care for her in the home she had on No. 42 Allen Avenue, Pasadena, California, and they were told the home would be theirs after she died, and they did receive it. So they came out in about 1947 or a little later but before 1951 when we came out as a married couple.

Aunt Lydia took care of Melissa so lovingly and gently. She said that she did for Melissa what she could not do for her own mom. (Interestingly enough, that happened again when I took care of Aunt Lydia for two and a half years later; at the same time, my family was taking care of our mom. I could not be in Ohio taking care of my own mother, but I am sure Mom felt this was a good thing.) Uncle Herman was different, and they certainly had their ups and downs, but I think they were somewhat companionable, and we enjoyed our time together when they had us over.

And New Year's Day was always special because before and after our children were born, we would put out chairs on the parade route for the Rose Parade with others they invited, and then we would enjoy the parade. The house was just two houses off the parade route on Colorado. Afterward, Aunt Lydia always had a nice dinner for us. Our children remember many wonderful times with Aunt Lydia—her backyard and the backyard picnics. The Chef Boyardee that she made her way, and they loved it. She was a very good cook. She was like a second grandmother to them.

When Aunt Lydia sold the home; much after Melissa died and Uncle Herman died, she thought she would move to Florida and "take care of her only brother." Well, hello, he was already pen-paling with lady number 3, and she saw the picture on the wall of it all and finally decided to come back to California and enter the Missionary Alliance Home in Santa Ana on Memory Lane and was there some years and loved it. She was kind of the greeter every time some new resident would come to live there. Then sometime later, before she began getting strokes, breaking bones, etc., I had to keep moving her from one room to the next care area and then to the final full care area, and she died there in 1987. The year my dear mom died, Aunt Lydia died the next month. She was very special and was loved by our family, and I was so glad to have her in California when we were new here.

I felt quite emancipated and very relieved that they both were out of their suffering through their dementia—I was always asking the Lord to take my mom "home," but it was not yet in his timing, and I worried about her a great deal since she was in Ohio, and I had to leave it to my brothers and sister to do what I could not do for her. They were wonderful in their care of her, and it lessened my worries about my mom. (There were only three of the six who had dementia—Aunt Marsie, my mom, and then, I feel because of strokes, Aunt Lydia. The rest were not affected.)

5. Florence Klotz. Born 1900. Died 1990. Dear Aunt Florence. First off, she marched to her own drummer, and I think she always did. She was so sweet, so very happy—not that she didn't have hard times in her life. Her husband died suddenly when the children were young. I adored Aunt Florence, and she was always laughing. Aunt Florence was a dear, sweet person to us and fun to be with. She loved to pound away on the piano. By the way, women wore girdles in those days; she didn't!

6. Esther Henrietta Klotz. Born 1904. Died 1991. Aunt Esther was a very interesting person. A strong person in that she worked at the Champion Sparkplug Company, and when the union came in, she refused to join and never did and was the last non-union member to retire many years later and still had not joined. She said the owner of Champion Sparkplugs came to see her personally, on the job, and thanked her for her beliefs that she stood by. She had her principles and did not believe in unions.

    She took care of Grandpa on Lodge Avenue till she got married—after he died. Grandpa didn't care for him because he put beer in his refrigerator, once! Aunt Esther and Aunt Lydia were both short and heavy set but always looked well groomed, etc. I don't know where they inherited that gene. The rest of the family did not have that problem—Aunt Marsie, maybe a little from living on the farm, etc. Before our wedding, these short aunts of mine were not introduced to my husband until after we were engaged. I guess I wanted him to know that I wouldn't end up with that look. I was young!

    Aunt Esther had a heart of gold and would do anything for anyone. She was active in church helping in many areas so willingly. (We all went to the Zion ME Methodist Church on, I think, Segar Street.) And both my father and mother's family belonged there, and I could sit with any cousin, aunt, uncle, or grandpa I wanted after Sunday school. Quite wonderful. Anyway, Aunt Esther married Irv (Irving), and they sold the family home of my grandfather's and moved near Reynolds Road in Toledo. He died some years later. He told me that years before he retired, he subscribed to *Reader's Digest* and put them all aside to read when he retired. I wonder if he ever did.

Then much later, Aunt Esther died of cancer—I think of the colon. She gave us some of her beautiful linen tablecloths she used for many church dinners in her home and lots of linen napkins. I so loved Aunt Esther for many reasons. For one, she was so special to ask me to be "her daughter" for a mother-daughter banquet at our family church, and that is a splendid memory for me. Thank you, Aunt Esther. Aunt Esther was also a "collector" and loved estate sales, and her attic was full of her treasures—I wonder if she ever used them. We all would have delighted in being asked to go up to the attic, but only my mother went with her. We thought it would be quite fun.

7. Elmer Klotz. Died at nine years of age—year? He had an illness that took him quite fast-childhood illness, I guess.

End of the line. All these women were remarkable in their own way. She loved her family very much, as did we. I wanted to tell a little about each because they were strong women and women of worth. They all loved the Lord and served him faithfully. They all did so much for others. That is what He asks of us.

My Mother's Correspondence

My father had many relatives in Vienna and Germany, and Mother corresponded with them soon after WWII was over to see what their needs were. You will see in the transcribed letters that they had many and were so grateful to receive anything. Along with food, my family sent snowsuits, shoes after they sent a paper pattern of size, and many other things of necessity. My mother and father would be pleased that we are now again in contact with many of the next generation and have been a part of gathering information for genealogy of the families.

Compassionate Caring

These are letters that came into my possession after my dear mother died, and I treasure them because it shows how much she cared about others that were hurting. This is immediately after World War II was over, and my dad had relatives in Vienna and Germany. During the war, these German relatives were considered "fighting against our country," but after it was over, there comes compassion.

These letters show how they hungered for so many items that they had to do without during the war years and prior to and after. Many had no one that could send them anything, but my mother sought them out to see where our family could help.

I understand from my cousin Marcia that other members in the family took responsibility for additional families that were related and sent them things to start the peace process of love again. These letters tell of them losing family members, always hardships, which all countries in Europe and Great Britain endured—doing without. My mother sent snow suits for the young ones. They sent an outline of the size of the foot of the child, and she bought shoes. They were so excited to get sugar, Nes for Nescafe/coffee, powdered milk, which they had not seen in so long, cinnamon, and raisins.

The letters went back and forth, and Mom and Dad responded to their needs and gave encouragement for their rehabilitation. We were amused when one of the later letters they were so hungry for "bon-bons," and Mom found some to send.

It does not matter what happens in life; it is the way you respond that matters. I was always taught that and so believe it. The letters attached are what I transcribed, and then a young woman from Germany helped. They were able to write, for the most part, in English and kept apologizing. However, we thought they did quite well in explaining things.

What I would have loved is to have some of the letters Mother sent to them. She often told about our family. I think these families thought we were wealthy, but in comparison, we were and even became richer for sharing what we had with them. Ruth Kuehnl Lampe, 8/12/09

LETTERS FROM GERMANY/VIENNA
Letter to My Parents from Relatives in Vienna Written on March 24, 1942

FROM: Emerich Jergitsch

My dear cousin Berthe (my mother Bertha),

It's a long time, I think twenty years, that we didn't hear from the other. I hope, my dear Berthe, you are going well with your husband and your children. *We, in Europe, had a very bad time, first with the Nazi and then with the war(Russia).* My dear son joined in the war in 1939, and so long time he was always away from us, and now it's already two years that we didn't hear anything from him. Sometimes, I am very zx, but I hope so much, and I beg to our dear God that my good boy come back. I have also two daughters, Gerta and Ericka. They have very nice husbands, and Ericka has three children. My dear father's death was in 1926; my mother's death was before in 1920. My brother

Wendelin killed himself in 1933, and Haus was killed by a bomb last year just before the war was finished.

The husband of Ericka is a physician, and I ask you, my dear, today if it would be good if he goes to America—could you do something for us please? Not financially, a position. Please write me if a doctor has a job/ need in North America. Have you perhaps somebody in New Zealand? There we like very much to go. Now, my dear cousin, how are you and your family? I know you are married, but I forget your married name, and I hope you will receive that letter. I am very curious where you live in the past years (?) How many children have you and what's the matter with all your brothers and sisters? If you could send me a little parcel, I would be very pleased and hope to have very soon an answer from you. I send you very much greetings for all your family with very much kisses.

I am your cousin,
Miti Jergitsch-Kuhnel, Austria

Letters, Not Long After WWII
Written on March, 28, 1947 (all mail censored after mailed)

EMERICH JERGITSCH

My dear cousin Berthe! (Bertha, my mother)

Thank you so much for your nice and long letter. I was very glad to receive it—spent time with Ericka and her children. It was a very nice time. I was so glad to see again my little children which I love so very much, especially Roswithea; we call her "Livita" or "Lweeta." She is a very clever child. In autumn, she will come to school, but now she knows already to write several words and to read light things in her children book. Dagi is a good child; she loves very much her mother; she is always with her, and the little boy, Rainer, is a funny boy. We laughed so much with him. He runs away everywhere, and one must be always behind him. Hartberg is a little town in Steierwark. It has three thousand inhabitants; my son-in-law, Gustav, is their physician at the hospital.

Last year, they had so much typhus there, and now it is warmer. It begins again in Hartberg. It is not allowed to drink water; we had always mineral water.

Emerich and I we are always in anguish that the children may receive this terrible illness, but I hope our good God will all do in goodness.

Now, I am again at home. I have very much to do. I am also alone for the house work, and you understand that the rooms and kitchen are quite dirty when a man is alone at home. My dear Berthe, you must have much to do to make all the work along in your great house. I know you have not much time to write letters. I will write to you as often as I can. Your letter was so interesting. You wrote all the little things which passed in a happy family from Ruth and Maria (Marie) when they are in your pretty bathroom with all the nice and new things and glasses to "make up" their young and beautiful faces, and you, my dearest, you are clearly a good and wonderful mother, and you are pretty through the love for your lovely children, isn't so, my dear Berthe?

Oh yes, I understand very well your German letter, and it is enough good for the long time you didn't write German letters, but please write your next letter in English because it is a good exercise for me if I came to Toledo to speak very well English. I am glad to hear that the picture from Erika enjoyed yourself, and I was happy that she looks like Florence and Marie.

Is Marie (Aunt Marie, my father's half sister) married? You said she lives in Michigan. Has she children? Now I enjoy myself in waiting for your parcel and for all the good things you will send to me; yes, we. It is very necessary; *now it is very bad in Austria.* It is so kind from you and George to send also a parcel to Gerta (?) and Ericka, and I thank you very much for all. Gerta's address is: Gerta Friedrich, Eibelstadt a. Main bei Wurzburg, Germany.

Gerta has a little boy. His age is eight months, and in October, she will have her second baby. It is a little bit too quick; the poor Gerta will have a hard time with two little children, and I can't help her *because it isn't allowed to travel to Germany.* Ericka will also write to you and give you the *measure of the shoes* from her children. *I beg you send her if you can,* perhaps you have old stockings and clothing from your children, and please ask the other cousins if they have several things from her children to send it to Gerta and Erika.

Erika knows very well to sew, and she can change all for her children.

Emerich has a wire factory; we thought always that our son, our dear Emerich, will have the factory, and old Emerich and I can travel and to Gerta and then to Erika and now? (Note: He died either in war or in some other way, perhaps in another letter.) We have great sorry where Emerich may be. In the long nights when I can't sleep, I always think where he is. And I beg so much to our good God that He may help me. I am very sorry to hear that your good father was so ill; he has zuckerkrauk (diabetes). My mother had the same illness, and I know how hard it is, and I hope so much that your dear father may be soon sound. I am very happy to receive soon several photos from your family. I am already very curious how you and George and your children look and your house and garden. *Yes, it would be so nice to be together in Toledo to drink coffee with milk and sugar; how much I love that; you haven't an idea.* And have a grand time with Berthe and George and all the other folks. I am sure we shall have this in two or three years.

Now, my dear, I sent all my love to you and George and your children. Please write soon.

Yours truly, cousin and friend.
I shall give different stamps on my
letter for your nice postman.

Maria

This letter is from Maria in Vienna to my mother and father. July 1947

(NOTE: *Some* she did on typewriter and then some written in German and some written in English, three pages—will do the best I can with this, Ruth)

My dearest cousin Berthe!

Today, I shall also try to write you on this machine, but it is not so good as yours because that is already an old system, but I hope you can read it. Your letter was very well written; one can

RUTH LAMPE

see you help in the office of your husband. When I was younger, I was also several times in the office from Emerich, but now my niece and several younger persons are there.

Dearest Berthe, don't be angry that I didn't immediately answer for your nice letter. First, I was in Hartberg, and when I came back, I had so much to do to run everywhere for having a passport to go to Germany. It is always a great pleasure for me to receive a letter from you. You are always telling me all the things from your family, which I like very much. It is interesting for me, and so I thank you very much for the last letter.

Yes, I would like so much to go to Herta; you know she will have her second child in October, and I hope it will be possible to go in September there to help her when she will be in the hospital. It's already two years that I haven't seen Herta and Georg and the little Jorg. I haven't seen at all.

Ya, it was a very nice time when Erika, Gustav, and Swita were here. We were in theater and circus and also in moving picture but Snowhite. We didn't see it in present. It is not to see in Austria. Erika saw it already in London in 1938.

Ja, I asked you for Wool to knit little dowers for Swita and Dagi, and if you can send me from that, it would be very kind of you.

(Then several paragraphs were handwritten in German regarding clothes for little children.)

It would be very, very nice of you to send me again a parcel. The last parcel was selected very good: Nes coffee, sugar, milk, rice, and all the other good things. If you can, we need powdered cinnamon. We like that so much in cookies.

It was interesting for me to hear that Therese was visiting you. Has she also children? Is she living in Toledo? And Caroline,

140

what is the matter with her? You wrote once, she is married; George has two brothers. The one has the office from Uncle Gustav, and he has seven children. I forget his name, and the second brother, where is he? Ya, Florence sent me a picture from Alice; she is a pretty girl.

(German) George looks like his father, and George looks like his brother

Franz. I hope my parcel will be soon at your house. I send you all my love, dearest, and best wishes to you and George also from Emerich.

Yours truly,

Cousin Maria

Hello to Marie, Ruth, George and Robert! (She also asks, "Who does your laundry and windows?")

(NOTE TO MARCIA: Wish I had the letters of our family that my mom wrote to her. My mother was such an interesting writer and tells of her "observances," and I think I take after her in that way—I am proud of that. My mother was such a dear, dear person and was always so loving to all she met and was so "equal" with her love to all her own children, and I never, never remember her scolding me or my brothers or big sister Marie. (I think Marie was such a wonderful help to her, and Marie talks about how she loved Mom so much because she was such a wonderful mother to her. And my father, also, always treated her in love and respect because of his own love for her but also out of respect of the promise Mom and Dad gave Marie's mother, Dad's sister Bertha.)

Marcia, this is a harder one, written in English, to read, I will try my best. It was written (clearer on envelope) by E. Zahonirek, Hartbeg, UV 98 Heiermark, Osterreich.

(Picking it up the best I can. I think you will eventually get the best of the letter to understand what they are saying.)

Hartberg, February 26, 1948

Dearest Bertha, dearest Uncle George,

We got yesterday your so great love, that wonderful parcel which contained so various good things. It has arrived in very well. Only the sugar parcel was broken, but the sugar still into the big box. It was a festive package below Erica. We and the cousins . . . so grateful, and everybody will soon eat immediately.

Thanks for your so great love! That parcel is a big help again for us.

Have you got our last letter? We shall send it with airmail. That we can be nice that it will arrive you.

And now a question about you concerning! Will come a new war? In our old Europe of lightens again and all our old anxiety, that Germans will, especially Berlin, become the occasion of a new war, seems become true. And the terrible in this thing is the fact that we don't know what will be better for us: a new war or peace time among the same conditions which we now have and money which we have to spend now (being devalued). You can thank God always for you to be able to live in America where to be American citizen. Our life in Europe and especially in Austria is in (chain?) of war, of poverty, and anxiety of a new war. (1948 may have war with Russia) All over . . . life eclipses so much of this terrible fact is so impossible to project anything. For instance (like?), we have plan in the next year to go back to Vienna for the beginning of my ordination(?) as doctor in the capital because we are citizens and don't work (want?) to spend our life in the provinces. Just it is nearly impossible for plan it if we like to Berlin. Nevertheless, what happen now, forever, can happen in the next . . . by us in Austria, and after we are seating in cage . . . fight as Russian soldier in the Russian army or to go as miner in the Russian uranium mines. Now you will . . . what will be better for us; the same peacetime conditions have now or a new war. I shall hope!

Please write us your . . . about the beginning of the next war and about the prospect of your new Presidential Candidate H. Wallace. Who will be better for us, Dewey or Wallace? Perhaps will be better a . . . as this terrible life, what we have now.

Please . . . once again, it is always a great joy if arrives a letter from you. Thousand thanks for your love! (Then some words in German.) And signed from sincerely (can't make it out).

Then a short note at bottom from Ericka in German. (German friend Anna read it to me, "Thank you very much for the wonderful package for everyone. Please send more shoes.")

Note to Marcia: If you want a copy of this, let me know.

MY MOTHER'S TREMENDOUS FRUSTRATION WITH "THE DRINK"

My mother wrote poems or letters in frustration regarding the operators of taverns. My dad's sometimes favorite place was called "Uncle's Inn." Mom wrote out of anxiety over what drinking did to, not only my father but to anyone. I think it is great that she kept a journal these times to express herself. My father's drinking was sporadic, and it came and went, but the worst was when I was about five or six years old, I believe. After that, it was, well, we could never tell, but it was not constant except during that time on Shasta Drive. His work was irregular for that period, and that must have worried him, but drinking is a poor excuse. I remember my grandmother came over, and I can still see her sitting on the piano bench and asking questions. I guess she wanted to see for herself and give us support and perhaps a "listen up" to our father.

Through it all, I had pain for my father. I don't think I talked about it with my brothers, at least I can't remember. It was a sad day when, after Mother made it plain that if he did not stop, she was going to take us and leave for Grandpa's house.

We walked the many blocks to Grandpa's home (maybe ten), and there we stayed for eight months. My brothers and sister adjusted, but I never did. I missed my daddy so much, plus I was a little first grader, and Mother would not let me walk some blocks to play with a schoolmate. It was too far, and I was too young. There were no young people in my grandfather's neighborhood.

My mother was my best friend, and I remember times of combing her hair and just being a part of her day that summer. Grandpa didn't like crying children, and that was hard, and I held that within me all those months. Waiting. At last, my mother and father told us that they have a home to rent, and we were going to move. That was good news, even though we had some semblance of peace while there at my grandpa's. He was a quiet, sweet Sunday school teacher of older men, and that gives a picture of him.

With the cherries we had in the backyard, dad used the "dregs" for wine he put in a cask down the basement. I clearly remember he went down the basement one man and came up another a short time later. Unbelievable. Oh, how I remember that. How drink reduces a person. Because of that, I was never interested in drinking, and I knew I would not marry anyone who had this problem. My mom got so frustrated that she went down and turned the spicket, and out it drained. We thought she might really get into trouble, but she didn't. Smelly old stuff. She was able to lay down the law when he was sober. Dad would always ask her the next day at breakfast, "How bad was I?" and she would always say, "You made a fool out of yourself again, and you can't be proud of that."

He was always so ashamed. If you knew him when he was sober, he was wonderful. He was strong, I thought very handsome, interesting in what he had to say, and enjoyed his family so much and show such love. That was so obvious. This always saddened me to see my father reduce himself to this, but desiring alcohol is a terrible weakness, and control over it is not easy. I think of all the young children that have to go through what we did, and it saddens me.

This father was still the special father that he was when not inebriated, and we learned to live with it and forgive, and Mother always saw that we had total respect for him. That saved the family. The kind of woman she was. Remarkable!

This is what my mother went through in her suffering in life, and she did it with strength in the Lord. Her walk was strong, and we saw that. She knew what a good man my father was, and she loved him. This suffering is what gave me strength in life with what I dealt with in my own marriage. My dear husband had something that he had no control over. It was genetic.

When I read him these stories, he has tears in his eyes, and he says, "Why couldn't I have had a mother like that?" These are such mysteries. I told him, "Someday you can talk to God about that." Ruth Kuehnl Lampe, 2012

Here are some letters and a poem Mother wrote when things were very serious in our family because of my father's drinking:

April 20, 1945

To the proprietor of Taylor's Café,

Do you *ever* stop to wonder what becomes of a man, loaded down with your wares when he leaves your place? Or how he treats his family when he comes staggering home? Or what is done to his *soul,* his morale? Or as you only interested in how many times the cash register rings? I'm wondering if you have such a *liberal supply* for all your customers.

The government has many uses for *alcohol* these days. There's a *war* on, remember? So don't try and dump your entire *quota* into one guy.

Signed, A Disgusted Wife.

P.S. My neighbors and friends have seen my husband enter your place entirely sober and leave it *hours* later many times, in a deplorable condition, so you can't deny this. Think it over.

We all have to give *account someday* for our *activities* here below. Can you face it?

The Poem. Dedicated to all the bottles on any café shelf.

"Truth is stranger than fiction."

Soldiers of destruction, standing in a row,
You are more destructive, by far, than any foe:
You boast that you give a lift to the people
And will send their spirits as high as a steeple.
The lift you give makes heads and hearts flutter,
But the kick you give sends them down to the gutter.
Your uniforms amber, your labels gold and green
And on your head caps with ripples are seen.
You look very restless as you stand in a row,
For within you, your spirits are revving to go.
To find some poor weakling, who himself can't define,
Who seeks through you, his worries to end?
Do you help him? Can you give him a lift?
A million times no, your destruction is swift.
Instead of feeling better, he feels far worse,
And soon he discovers a *flat, empty purse.*
Your mission is finished, your present work done,
And you stand at attention to snare some other weak son.

(P.S. I'm not a member of the Anti-Saloon League, but I sure believe in *sane drinking.*) Signed BEK

MY FATHER'S FAMILY

H is father, *Joseph Gustav Kuehnl* (Kuhnel, German way of spelling *U*, with two dots over it, indicates ue.)

Joseph Gustav was born in Aupersheim bei Teplitz in Bohemia, Austria (Bohmen) in 1862.

He died in Toledo, Ohio, on October 2, 1923, at the age of sixty-one. He is buried in Forest Cemetery, Section W1, Grave 2, Lot 364. (When my daughter Beth and I visited the grave site in 2006, we laid flowers on his grave, and I mediated on how much my father loved him, and all his family, and how I would have loved knowing him.)

His father was Franz Haver Kuhnel. His mother was Maria Kuhnel nee Honigertuss (SIC), born in Nicklasberg in Bohemia. They were the owners of steam-powered mills (Dampfmuhlen) in Aupersheim bei Teplitz. These mills produced flour. The family is thought to have been of considerable wealth. Gustav was one of several children born to Franz and Maria. Other children were Wendelin, Franz (Fank), Julius, Joseph, and Paulina. Grandfather's brother, Wendelin, established himself in Vienna as an architect/builder, and many of his descendants still live there. He was very wealthy and owned the "famed" Villa Kuhnel (picture) which was originally built for the emperor of Austria—Franz Josef and his wife, but in the end, the wife did not want to live there, and so Franz Josef sold it to Wendelin at a greatly reduced price. (I had other information, and I do not know if it agrees with what Marcia has found out, that during WWII, the family was expelled from the house, and Nazi officers took over, not hard to understand but don't know the full truth of it. RL)

My grandfather, Gustav, immigrated to America (at the age of eighteen) after his brother Franz (Frank) came. Franz (Frank Kuehnl) immigrated to America before Grandfather Gustav. His descendents are in Portland, Oregon. Julius was a banker in Karlsbad, Bohemia. Grandfather Gustav was one of the younger children. It was noted in the family history that he converted from Catholic to Protestant faith in America at the age of nineteen. (Aunt Alice has told me that someone told him about Purgatory taught in the Catholic Church, and he wanted "none of that stuff.")

Grandfather Gustav made several visits to Austria, the last one being, perhaps, ten years before his death. His given name was Gustav; his baptismal name was Joseph. For business and legal purposes in America, he was J. G. Kuehnl, Joseph G., or Joseph Gustav Kuehnl. Friends and relatives referred to him as Gus or Gustav. Especially, he was Gustav in Austria as he had a brother Joseph.

My father's mother came from La Crosse, Wisconsin. Her name was Elise (Lizzie) Schwarz. She was born in 1869, the daughter of Charles Schwarz of La Crosse, Wisconsin. They married when she was eighteen, and he was twenty-five years old and had five children; two died as infants (Julius and Henry). Gustav and Lizzie were married about sixteen years when Lizzie died as a result of pregnancy complications after the birth of baby Henry in Toledo, Ohio. She was thirty-two when she died in April 1903. Aunt Alice told me that Grandfather was reading to her from the Bible, and she said, "Be still; Jesus is coming." And she died.

Elise had two sisters, Emma and Anna. (I think this was the Aunt Emma that I remember so well from my early childhood days; she was a beautiful gray-haired lady that would sometimes help my mother on Glynn Court with all of us when we were young. Also, our Aunt Alice came to help when she was in high school.)

According to a diary, it has been determined that Anna lived in Toledo with the Schmidt family, her aunt and uncle, while she was young. Elise came to visit her sister there when Elise was fifteen. Anna married a Mr. Smith and lived in Tecumseh, Michigan. They had four children: John Smith of Toledo, Arthur Smith of Detroit, Michigan, Helen Brazee, and Florence Leutheuser. (Somerset Michigan Leutheuser family where relatives operated all four corners, and we loved to visit there. One corner, there was a grocery store with a postal office in the back. Another corner had a gas station; another corner had a small hotel and the last corner had a John Deere dealership and new car dealership). Sister Emma married a Mr. Jones and lived in Chicago, Illinois. They had no children.

It is assumed that Gustav and Lizzie eventually resided in Toledo because of the relatives Lizzie had in the area.

His history also said that he worked for the government in resettling families out West who homesteaded to get the property. He seemed to go from Portland, Oregon, to Toledo or thereabouts. My father was born in Portland, Oregon. It was noted that in the assisting of homesteading people to the West, during the existence of the Homestead Act of the late 1800s, Gustav *probably* worked for the U.S. government by filling trains with homesteaders bound for the West. He may have earned as much as $100 a day, and he owned a homestead himself in Portland, Oregon. (My aunt notes that this was lost in a swindle in the early 1900s.) My aunt, in her historical records, noted that he and Lizzie broke up housekeeping seven times to move west with their children.

My father had two sisters from his parents. His mother died when he was nine years old.

Aunt Theresa (Aunt Tracy) was married to Uncle Fred and had one son, Dick. They lived on Green Street, a few blocks from the store and family home for years before moving to the west end of Toledo and then much later moved close to Heatherdowns in the south end in a smaller home. She was a strong and very attractive lady, educated in her own fashion. (Not in advanced schooling; in those days, you usually went to the eighth grade. However, her husband, my uncle Fred, has graduated high school.)

She was a leader in strength and purpose, and women looked up to her because she had strong beliefs.

She was such a favorite, and I wanted to be like her, all my life. She was very special to me in so many ways. When we had our cottage, she and Uncle Fred spent many days with us there, and we had such fun, especially taking walks and sitting out in the swing, having fun family conversations or just talking about things that were interesting. She let me stay at their home with them when I was first dating Rol, and everyone else was at the cottage, and that was special being in their home with them and very special that it was their son who knew Rol and introduced us. And we went on our first blind date, double dating with Dick and Marge.

Aunt Tracy and Mom and I also went to Detroit, to Hudson's department store (my choice) to pick out my wedding dress, and I tried the wedding dresses on for them, and that was so special. She also gave me a bridal shower, something about entertaining that she did so well. She was a very refined lady that knew the proper things of life. She was a very special friend to my mom and loved her brother, my dad. Her life helped give me direction as did all the women of both my mother and father's family. They had a certain something that made me proud of them.

Aunt Bertha, my sister Marie's mother. (And then she was a big part of our family.) She died when Marie was six weeks old but must have been loved very much by my mother and father because they took the responsibility of raising her at her dying mother's request (because Marie's father had other children, and she thought Marie being a bit sickly that she would be better having them raise her rather than her real father taking on the responsibility of a child that would add extreme burdens since she needed a lot of care in the early year). She lived with my parents from infant to eleven months and then came back at three years and was with us till she got married.

Our family considered Marie our sister and always have, but legally, she was never adopted by my parents because her natural father would not allow that to happen, but she took our last name as her own from school age on (her request, less confusing).

Our grandfather then married a wonderful woman by the name of Maria Caroline Kettemann on January 13, 1904, at the age of forty-two.

They had five children: Marie Barbara, Florence, Harold, Caroline, and Alice. She died on December 19, 1940, in Toledo, Ohio, at sixty-five years of age. She is buried in Forest Cemetery, Section W1, Grave 3, Lot 364) (further information below regarding each one as I remember them or was told, RL)

OTHER INTERESTING FACTS ABOUT MY GRANDFATHER:

My grandfather had quite a history. He sold Coney Island hot dogs in Chicago, owned a saloon in La Crosse, Wisconsin, and owned a butcher shop in La Crosse, Wisconsin. My aunt Caroline also stated that he was a friend, or at least an acquaintance, of William Cody (Buffalo Bill), probably during his homesteading the West period or during the time of selling his medicines at Medicine Shows, perhaps.

He had invented several medicines and sold them through the mail. It is not quite accurately documented if it was something he invented or took on from someone else and sold the medicines. Aunt Caroline's records showed he owned a patent medicine business in Toledo for many years. The knowledge of the preparation of medicines was learned in Europe prior to his coming to the U.S. The name of the company was the Stomatone (for stomach, liver, and kidneys) and Bohemian Mineral and Celery (Sprudelselzer). It is said that he lost the license and let it go when he became busy with the store, and Bromo-Seltzer took it. The medicine was made in the home in the "medicine room." This was the job of Bertha, the eldest child (my sister Marie's birth mother).

At the first Toledo residence, 225 City Park Avenue, the medicine room was located to the rear of the house. The printing of the labels, etc., was done in the barn.

At the second Toledo Residence, 45 City Park Avenue, the medicine room was off the main dining room, and the printing was done in the basement.

Grandfather Gustav traveled with his products to other cities. He also filled orders sent by mail from as far away as Denver, Colorado, and did business in the Toledo area as well.

J. G. Kuehnl fancy Groceries and Meats, 45 City Park Avenue was located just east of Toledo's German community on Lenk's Hill. The store came about through a $2,000 inheritance from Austria and the desire not to travel so much with the medicine business. The store began as a sideline to the medicine business until the grocery store became established. And I understand he gave it up when the work of the grocery store took much of his time, and he could no longer keep up with his producing and marketing the medicine.

The structure was built in about 1908 by Mr. Rorbacher, a builder of that day. It consisted of a store which faced City Park Avenue and an attached five-bedroom home which faced Green Street. A barn and stable were also located on the property off Green Street. The home had a library on the second floor which contained many first-edition books. Here is where Grandfather Gustav, a very religious man, held his own personal daily devotions and Bible reading every morning at ten.

Aunt Alice also told me that because the library was above the store, and that is where he knelt and had "audible" prayers, you could hear him in the store. (I was told that my father, when he came home from WWI, wanted to know exactly what time his father had his devotions. It was important to him to know that about his father. My father also believed very much in prayer.) We have one of the printer blocks for labels—our daughter Beth has it, and it tells the ingredients.

My father's father married again. She was a dear woman who Uncle Adam, her uncle from Michigan, sponsored to come over from Germany. She was a wonderful stepmother to my father, and he loved her very much. My father cried when the call came to him that she had died after a lengthy illness, and I remember that day so plainly, seeing such painful grief. They had five children themselves, and she also helped run the family grocery store, but I never heard my father talk about anything that would lead me to think he did not love all his family. I truly think it was because they got such strengths in love and faith from their parents. He loved his father very much, and his father loved him, and that was a strong bond.

The age order of this second family was Marie, Florence, Harold, Caroline, and Alice.

Aunt Florence Kuehnl. A strong woman; my dad "vented" many things to her, I think, when he was inebriated because he thought she could take it. Besides, I think they had a close bond. Aunt Florence was single for a lot of years and ended up by marrying "the boss" she worked for at a large wholesale hardware business (Bostwick & Braun) in downtown Toledo—I believe Summit Street, and they lived in a lovely home in Old Orchard. Uncle Bob had an adopted son from his first marriage, and his name was Dick Shannon, and he was just a few years older than I was, and I saw him in high school once in a while. However, years later—after children and a failed marriage and then a marriage to a woman that looked older but seemed so content with her—she seemed very simple and plain for what his tastes were before, perhaps through her, he became a strong Christian with living daily for the Lord. What a change from a materialistic looking guy to later owning a small sandwich shop and enjoying the simple life.

Aunt Florence had strong faith, I believe, because the strong faith of her father and mother influenced all the children a great deal. She was amusing and lots of fun at family gatherings when Uncle Harold and Aunt Phyllis got us all together for later. Aunt Florence must have loved my father and respected him because she was with us each step of the way in my father's final illness and was also an encourager to get him to the heart specialist and even called her own specialist, Dr. Koebacher (his family owned Tiedtke's, I was told).

Aunt Florence died of breast cancer. It was a long and lingering illness, and she did not want to see family other than Aunt Tracy. They even took her by small plane to a healer in the Appalachian Mountains. (Or was it the hills of Kentucky?) I have been told, but that did not help. She was a good person, and I thought a great deal of her. After my father's funeral service, she arranged to have the whole family over to their home for dinner and to be together. This to me is love. I hope my father knew that somehow. I believe he did.

Aunt Carolyn Kuehnl. I called her Aunt Caroline. My middle name is Carolyn, and I do not know if I was named after her, but I would like to think I was. Aunt Caroline was very special. She and Uncle Dick represented family to me in as much as they were always there for you (family)—in my later years. Any event of the family, she and Uncle Dick were there; every funeral, wedding, giving a bridal shower for Marge and Dick Haas at their home. All these things I remember of her and her sweet smile and caring ways in listening as was Uncle Dick.

I have a wonderful picture of her behind the grocery store counter where she helped wait on the customers. She was a historian of the family and knew and remembered and researched many things that have been helpful to me now. And she would be pleased to know Marcia and John; two of their children are doing much more with the genealogy and even connecting with family again in Vienna. With the kind of love that she had, I somehow knew she stood by my father in the way that she could. That was enough for me.

My father never had anything but love for his family. This too came from the strengths that he got from growing up with a loving father and his own mother and then his beloved stepmother that took special note of him always and gave him as much love as she had time for. Thank you, Aunt Caroline, for all you meant to me.

Aunt Marie Kuehnl. Aunt Marie and Uncle Glenn were a joy to be around. I loved visiting when they lived on City Park Avenue across from the store. I remember they had me over (I think) for an overnight with Carol and Marilyn, and it was such a special family time. They were so kind and loving as a family, and it was a joy to see, and they showed me such love. When they moved to Jackson, Michigan, when the girls were in high school, we went to visit them in their home there several times, and Aunt Marie had us all for dinner a couple of times, and it was wonderful being together. I was in Carol and Don's wedding, and Carol and Marilyn were in our wedding. Special times being with them at those festivities and family joy. Aunt Marie and Uncle Glenn had a lot of love to give because they loved one another, and it showed. Thank you, both, for showing me that kind of love.

Aunt Alice Kuehnl. "The California Girl!" Aunt Alice was the youngest and danced to another tune in what she wanted in life, which was not at all bad, just different. Her sisters were pretty grown when she was still young, and her father died also when she was young. I don't know a lot of what she did between those years and the years she chose to go into the ministry and was friends with Kathryn Kuhlman and also attended the Angelus Temple in Los Angeles to study to be a pastor. She told me later that it became clear to her, after preaching, that that was not the road God wanted her to travel.

She was very involved, for years, in the Four Square Church. She told me, and we got to know one another quite well, as well as you could, I guess. Rol and I came out to California after we married to live, and we saw them once in a while and in her later years were involved in many ways. She said that when her mother got so ill and was bedridden, her family asked her if she would leave her schooling in Los Angeles and come home and care for their mother. She was the only one able to do that because she was without family. So she did, and she said that time was very special to her, and she cared for her dear mother with much love.

After she died, I know Aunt Alice lived on Dorr Street in the house that Aunt Florence bought before her marriage, and then I believe she left again for California. Things I remember about Aunt Alice: she was a wonderful storyteller of small instances that happened and told it in such a way, like the plumber coming and fixing something, that you laughed and laughed. She entertained us with other friends for dinner, and she was a very excellent cook. The very first Thanksgiving dinner I ever cooked completely (with phone help from my aunt Lydia, my mother's sister who lived in Pasadena), we invited Aunt Alice, Drake, and new baby Roxanne, and we had a nice day together.

I have to say that, being away from my own mother's wonderful cooking and having to fare for myself—and I always liked helping Mom and baking pies and cakes, etc.,—that was an astonishing success as a meal, and I was so full that, after they left, I lay down on the bed, stretched out, and said, "Don't move me."

I was so delightfully full of my delicious meal that I couldn't move. Aunt Alice worked most of the time, and we didn't see them too often, nor did we talk on the phone. In later years, I took cakes for her birthday, and she loved that. She now lives a quiet life as she is older. She died at ninety-four, I believe. All of the above, I had reason to believe from my aunt as she told me. She loved to talk about the family past.

Then my father had a stepbrother, *Uncle Harold,* and he was such a kind man. He worked hard in taking over the grocery store, and we got a kick out of all that he had piled in the store to sell. We enjoyed looking at it through my father's eyes. He took us to visit several times. He was proud of Uncle Harold doing well in providing for his very large family in a strong

Christian way. He was married to Aunt Phyllis who was a gem of a person and showed genuine love for everyone. Uncle Harold was a good man. We respected him for that.

I did not have much contact with my cousins because I moved to California to live after we were married in 1951, but it was always so nice when I did hear from them or saw them. Relatives are relatives. They are always yours and part of your life, and their life and happiness gives joy in just knowing that. I am happy that I have Cousin Marcia Kramp Roby to help me in my remembering parts of the family life that were blank spots for me.

Thank you, Lord, for allowing me to be a part of this wonderful family that gave strengths to me without even knowing it.

Much of this information is from history compiled by Aunt Caroline, her daughter Marcia, and Aunt Tracy in 1979 to 1980.

A footnote: My daughter, Beth, and I made a visit to Toledo in 2006 and revisited many places from the past as she was so interested in everything. Beth and I visited Forest Cemetery and sat for some time at the grave site of my grandmother Lizzie who we never knew because my father was only nine when she died. Violet lived only two hours and died in my father's arms. My father was sitting in the rocking chair, holding his first child, and baptizing her. He then had to bury her without my mother in attendance because she was so ill. How hard for our father to have his own first child, a daughter named Violet, and then laying her to rest in the same grave site as his mother. Violet was a perfectly formed baby, and there was no apparent reason why she died.

Baby Violet was born at home, and what they called a "quack" doctor left my mother to almost hemorrhage to death. None of the rest of us were born at home after that.

I truly felt the "presence" of my dad's grief at this grave site. I know how much my father loved all of us. In our Sister Violet's memory, I was encouraged in my heart to have her name added below her grandmother's name on the gravestone, just "Baby Violet—1921." My parent's first child who died at birth, my sister Violet, was also in that grave site, her coffin sitting on top of her grandmother's coffin.

It gave me peace and joy at the same time. In talking to the gravedigger, he said he did not know if they allowed two names on a gravestone years ago—it doesn't matter; it is there now.

These are family facts as I was told.

Life Moves On,

well lived, and then walking into the arms of Jesus.

Memories of our life on Marlowe Road. The war was over on two fronts by the middle of 1945. Dad was able to get back into building construction soon after. He had been in large construction in Toledo before the Depression, and now, he had to start with houses because that was the need at that time. It soon took off into larger things, and Dad had George and Bob involved also.

Many things changed in our family after moving to Marlowe Road. I was a junior in high school when we moved into our new home. My father continued to be very busy from 1945 until the end of 1948. (And he must have done quite well because my mother was able to live on what their savings had grown to besides the construction business, but that was only for a little more than three years, and all this was because they saved three out of four checks during the Depression.)

At the end of 1948, my father was told he only had a year more to live because of a heart condition. This proved to be true. This story is told in diagnosis is not good!

In January of 1949, George and Bonna got married. They built a new home in Toledo on Elmhurst and raised their children there until they made a move to Coronado in Toledo. They lived there many years. He passed away in November of 2009. Bonna now lives in Sarasota, FL.

Dad's last year was a thing of family. Dad did have one year, and it proved to be so special as I have written in *the Final Diagnosis* in this section. Dad died on December 7, 1949, and it was a sad time—very sad. Mother was again our leader and grieved well. I learned a lot by that. The only ones home now were Mom, Bob, and myself. The house was becoming quiet.

Before Dad's death, he encouraged the boys to take over and keep the business and told them "they could do it." And they did. They started small and waited patiently until their own reputation was established and then became very successful not only in building but buying land, building on it, and then leasing or selling the building. Dad would have been proud.

One of the wonderful things my brothers had going for them is their love and respect for one another. They always had this and never argued. Bob was out in the field, and George was working the office with getting new business, keeping the jobs going from the office and investing.

It was unfortunate that my dad never got to meet Rol, the man I married. I know they would've had a high regard for each other, and Dad would have been happy for me.

I met Rol on July 1, 1950, and it was so special from then on. (See other information on Rol.) I was going to the University of Toledo at that time—or rather in the fall—and we dated often. But then in December, he moved to California with Brother Royce. He kept writing me and eventually asking if my mother and I could come out to California for a visit, and she could be visiting her sister, and we could stay there. We dated every day, and then on July 1, 1951, we became engaged, and on November 22, 1951, we were married. All this beautiful love story was written up in my first book, *Surviving Mental Illness.*

In the meantime, Bob and Dolores made plans to be married on July 14, 1951. Mom and I had plans to return to Toledo, and Bob and Dolores were married, and it was beautiful as was George and Bonna's before them. They had a wonderful, full life, and Bob too passed away in March 2007.

Soon, mother would be all alone in our home, but I think she was happy to have the quiet in her life (except for the business because she willingly did the books for my brothers and kept them going in that way). That was a special time for her—but quiet.

There is so much I did not know about the time Mom was living by herself. One of the things I did not know till later was that she never could have her dinners in the breakfast room anymore because the rest of us were all gone, and it was too lonely to be there by herself. We all have to adjust, but it was sad for me to learn this. But my mother was strong and could do it. She loved being in the church choir and was a regular member every Sunday.

Mother eventually went into dementia, and we waited as long as we could until we put her in a home to be taken care of. It was hard on all of us—very hard, but this was the safest place for her, even though she lived to be almost ninety-four.

All those days are now gone, but the memory remains forever. I shall never forget our life together as a family. George and Bob are gone now, and Marie is not doing well and is living in a home for assisted care. Where has the time gone? Thank you, Lord, for the memories I now live with. Each one in my family made a fullness to my life, complete and overflowing with love.

Many things changed in our family after moving to Marlowe Road.

I am married and have lived in California for the past sixty years.

My father died when he was fifty-five, and my mother did not die till she was ninety-three.

Final days of my sweet, gentle mom.

She was in a convalescent home for some years before she died. None of us wanted her to be there, and the family tried everything to keep her in her own home. There was a woman across the street that my family hired to come in every day to watch over her, but it was already too late for my mother to understand that. She just could not make sense of how this woman got in the house, and she would peek on her, and the lady would peek on my mother. Lost cause.

Many things were done to keep her in her home. My brother George would stop by every day to check on her. My family, who lived in Toledo, would take dinner to her every day and would each eat with her, so they knew she was eating, and George would put out her medicines for the week in a daily reminder container. One day, he put up her Christmas tree, and when he drove by our home the next day, she had taken it down. My family took off all the knobs on the stove because she had a habit of putting her hand on each burner before going up to bed to check if they were off. They were afraid she would burn herself, so they hid the stove knobs.

My mom started going downhill rather abruptly in the summer of 1971 (78). She stopped writing letters (have some correspondence to verify this) and her memory was not good. (I was told she had said that she was so afraid of getting the grandchildren's names mixed up.) And she was quite senile/borderline at Beth's wedding in 1975. We placed Mom in the "home" when she was eighty-eight after trying to keep her in her own home till that was impossible.

George and Bob and I had a hard time with this. A mother that would do anything in the world for us all our life and we had to do this—for her own safety. However, knowing my mother, I know she would have said, if she could, "You did what you had to do, and I forgive you because you are still caring for me in doing this." I knew my mother well enough to know that she would realistically look at the situation, and if Dad would have needed this, she would have had the same attitude.

When I visited Mom and family in Toledo the last time I was staying with Mom in the family home, and that was usually yearly, I told my family that they should just stay away, and I would do everything for her so that would give them a break. Well, they gave me one of the stove knobs, and when I made my first breakfast, she stood close to me and kept saying, "But how did you make that heat up?" I had many answers for that.

I was nervous when I was there because she really didn't know me anymore, and it felt so strange. In my nervousness, I made breakfast so early, cleaned up the breakfast nook and kitchen, and had her sitting in her chair. By nine o'clock, she got up from her chair, and I asked where she was going, and she said to start breakfast. I gave her a second breakfast. From then on I made breakfast when she was ready.

She would usually take a nap in her favorite chair for about twenty minutes, and I would be sitting on the sofa next to her chair, quilting. She would be awake for about twenty minutes, and in that time, she would say things like, "Does your mother live near you?" I would look at her and smile and point to her, saying, "You, you are my mother," and she would respond, "Pardon me." And I would repeat that again, and then she would rub her head and say, "Maybe so, a lot of things get by me these days."

Another time, she woke up and said, "Do you have children, and do they live near you?" How hard it is to have a mother that loved your children so and not remember them. But she was so loveable during those days, and I was able to understand her.

Before her complete decline, my mother and I had a conversation in something that happened when I was a little girl, and she had never said anything before about it. But she pulled her chair over close to mine. (This is probably the last normal thing she said before she went into full dementia.) It was like she was waiting to clear that up before her days were over—always the loving mother—and she asked me, "Do you remember . . ." I looked at Mom and thought, *And she has carried these thoughts of protection all my growing-up years and then some.* And then I said to her, "No, Mom, I don't remember." It was something a little neighbor boy tried to do. He was being naughty in exposure in the side of the house. "His mother was devastated," Mother said. This was said so she could know I did not carry it with me all my life. Just between you and me, Mom. I love you so much for caring about me that much. Then you left us, and your memory was gone. One last thing you had to do as a mother.

Because we, as a family, felt she was not safe in her own home anymore, we had to make a decision for her. When she was in her late eighties, we had to put her in a home, and it was so hard on my brothers, George, Bob, and I and Marie. The three of us took her to the home George had chosen, and she seemed to surmise what was happening, and when we got there, she would not get out of the car, and George went in to get help.

They came out for her and encouraged her to come in, and she did, reluctantly. We left her after a bit and came back that night and found she had been sitting in the same chair that whole time, refusing dinner, with purse in lap, ready to go home when we got there. It was such a hard, hard time for us. A mother who would do anything for us, and we ended up doing this to her. There was no one in charge around, and that was not good because as we walked down the hall after our goodbyes, she seemed to understand and was following us, saying softly, "How could you do this to me?" Oh, the pain we felt.

It was quiet in the car going home with our own memories.

Because of the poor care but yet in a nice place, we moved her to another home close by because we were not satisfied with that home, and the new one was so much better for her. She was going downhill, and they treated her well and showed her much love. Families can be grateful for that.

The morning of January 2, 1987, the home called my brother's home to say she had died. My sister-in-law called me to tell me, and that was not enough for me. I had to talk to the one who was with her. They wrote a note also, and it said, "Bertha's final minutes were very quick. We had gotten her up as normal in preparation to eating breakfast. She was sitting up by the nurses' desk and was talking." (One said singing, and I believe that could be because Mom was in the choir for years.) She said, "She usually sat there in her wheelchair before meals. When she became quiet, the nurse looked over at Bertha, noticing that she appeared too quiet. She was already dead."

The letter she sent me also told me that the physician signed the death record as a massive stroke. The nurse ended it by saying, "I thank you for your kind words. Bertha was very special to us all and a privilege to care for." Sweet peace at last.

There were some funny moments. Once when I went home to Toledo to visit Mom and the family, Brother Bob and I drove out on a Saturday to see Mom. All the patients were lined up in the hall, on both sides, with their heads down as they napped. I went up to Mom and did as I always did when I went to see her. I hugged her and said, "Hi, Momma, this is Ruthie, and I have come to see you" and then gave her smooches.

It was very quiet, but I heard Bob behind me saying, "Ruth, that isn't Mom?" I stood up straight to digest that, and then he said, "I thought it was Mom also, but Mom is over there!" So I went to the other side of the hall and did the same thing to my unresponsive mom, and she never woke up. When I looked around and looked at that little lady I awakened; her eyes were open wide, and she was probably thinking, "What just happened here?" We laughed and laughed all the way home. What a mistake not knowing your own mother.

It was hard on all of us as she became more and more in another world, her world of youth and younger years. I finally gave it all to the Lord and knew He was taking care of her, his faithful servant, even in this time of her life.

She was, as long as I can remember, sitting in her chair in the living room with her Bible and study materials, and you just knew where she got her strength. Words were not needed. We saw with our own eyes what made the difference in this woman's life. Such a beautiful, quiet faith.

DIAGNOSIS NOT GOOD!

It probably was about December 1948. I was eighteen when we got the devastating news that our father had perhaps one more year to live. We knew his health was not good—he knew it was not good! But because of that, he was putting off going to see a specialist because of the news he might be told. He was only fifty-four, a young man by standards of today.

One of his sisters kept saying to him, "George, you just have to see a doctor!" and of course, my mother had been urging him to do this for quite some time. His pat answer was "soon, I plan to go to Ann Arbor to the University Hospital and get a full checkup." Good plans, but no action put behind them.

Finally, Aunt Florence, his sister, said, "George, I am going to make an appointment for you at the heart specialist we go to. He is really not taking on any more new patients, but I know I can convince him to take you as a patient." Now, he had no escape plan. The dye was set. The appointment was made.

As a family, we were all anxious. Our father was a heavy smoker of heavy-duty Lucky Strike cigarettes and also had an off and on drinking problem, which only flared up once in a while and not constant. All these things were causing his body to react in various ways, and they were not good.

His visit to the doctor consisted of his first being observed by the doctor through a two-way mirror as he watched his shortness of breath and all the other mannerisms of someone with a heart condition and fluid buildup.

He gave him a thorough examination, and I will remember it always as he walked in the front door. He said, "Dr. Koebacher said I have no more than a year to live and went as far as to say what time you have will be a gift because you are virtually a walking dead man that has not taken good care of himself."

This news was not good; however, we had to accept it. We loved Dad so much, and we wanted to encourage him in whatever way we could. But instead of encouraging him, he was an encourager to us in the way we lived his final year.

How liberating it was to have him in the hands of a good doctor; how liberating it was to know that he could not take another drink; how liberating it was to know that he would not be allowed to smoke, but how hard it was to think we had just one year left with him.

It probably was the very best year and certainly a wonderful gift from God we ever had because he was always joyful, always was a good storyteller, and that was a joy, always interested in what the menu was for our dinner, knowing he could not have any of it. In the evenings, we sat around as a family, and he would do things like peel an apple and pass the pieces around to us to enjoy.

It was so peaceful, so unbelievably peaceful.

My mother and father usually went down to Florida in January for a couple of weeks' vacation, and the doctor allowed him to go again, but my brother Bob was going with them to do the driving. Mother wrote a journal of that vacation, and how I love it, knowing everything they did. They were at peace. My mother and father had peace again without the drinking and disruptions that brought. That must have brought so much joy to my mother. I know it did to us.

He lived a peaceful year with peace in his heart. You could tell.

He had a few times that the ambulance was called, and he had to have a few days in the hospital, and how he hated that. He did not like the stern twenty-four-hour nurses and being away from home or being in the large oxygen tent that they used to use.

Life went on because he wanted it that way. I remember coming in from a date and was being very quiet because we went out for hamburgers after the weekend dances, and once, when I looked up to the top of the stairs, after avoiding the third step that creaked, I saw my father standing there with a lighted match, saying, "Thought you would like to see better!" I loved that.

Never a reprimand because both my mother and father knew we all were trustworthy and would not do anything that they would not like.

In October, Dad ordered a new car because his intent was to go down to Florida again in January, with Bob driving. That was not to be. His doctor called my mother in and said, "If George makes it down to Florida, he will never make it back—his time has almost arrived."

He must have surmised this himself because he said one Sunday in December, "I think I am going to ask the doctor to put me in the hospital for a full checkup before we go to Florida." *He knew; he knew!*

I went with Dad that Sunday and sat with him while Mom checked him in. It was a special time of being with him. Someone who loved me so much, and I loved him. He was my strength.

That became his last week on earth. Every night, we spent the night in the Solarium, close to his room. All us kids, Mom, and several of his sisters, and we took turns going in to see if he was sleeping or at least resting well. When I went in one night, he opened his eyes and saw I had tears flowing down my cheeks. (Every day, we were told he would not last another night, but he would rally around.) He said, "What's the matter, honey, don't you feel well?" Dad, not me—it is for you. But he knew. My brother George tells of how Dad talked to him about he and Bob carrying on the business,

171

even though they were in their early twenties and said, "George, I know you and Bob can do it—you are prepared."

On the day he died, in the morning, Mother was sitting in the chair in the corner. He awakened and said, "Bert (for Bertha), you look so tired. I want you to go home and get some rest because there is no sense with both of us being down, and the children need you." She did go home and took a little nap on the sofa. It was not long, and she felt this light shaking of her shoulder, and she said it was her long gone father, and he said, "Bert, get up and get back to the hospital; it is time." She did, and when she was going down the hall, the nurse was motioning her to hurry, and she went into his hospital room, and he was waiting for her with his arm and hand stretched out, and she took it, and then he was gone. Thank you, Lord, for that precious gift of farewell.

I have never stopped missing my dear father. He was strong, tall, and very good looking with blue eyes and a wonderful personality that had a lot of joy in it.

Mother was so strong in her faith and took it so well, and it gave us direction in how to accept things in life. A strong memory.

After my father had been dead for about five months, Mother had a dream that he came to her and said, "Bert, I want you to go look for a cottage to buy so that the family can keep together." He was always thinking of us. My mother felt that so strongly that when she looked in the paper the next day, there was an ad for a cottage at Vineyard Lake that sounded so perfect. She called the realtor, and that late afternoon—or the next—Bob, Mom, the realtor, and me drove to Vineyard Lake and found this perfect red and white cottage that slept many and was so precious with large windows that opened up to the lake and a huge dining table to serve a lot of people and a precious living room of blue wicker furniture with colorful cushions. It had a front yard with swings to sit in and ponder the day. It was perfect. And Mother said, "I want to purchase this cottage." And she did.

God has been so real in our life, always, and this was the perfect gift that Dad could give us, and it was enjoyed for years and years.

Thank you, Lord. You are so faithful.

Ruth Kuehnl Lampe, March 2009

This is me in one of Janette's complete hand-me-downs. Maybe 3rd or 4th grade. Off that porch railing my Brother's jumped using an Umbrella. I tried it once!

TYPED FROM MOM'S WRIT TEN LAST "WILL" TOLEDO, OHIO—JUNE 27, 1968

To my dear children, George, Robert, Ruth, and Marie,

Recently, I have reviewed the "will" made out between your father (deceased, December 7, 1949) and me made out during his last illness, and I decided I needed to correct some things and add other provisions.

Because we loved our children dearly, we both worked hard to provide a happy future for our dear ones. I'm sure you will agree.

Our innermost wish is that you will all be true to God and His beloved Son Jesus and will always bear in mind that the church is the house of God, and as Christians, we must not stay away but give it our full support, financially and in service.

The world has many things to offer—some good and many destructible, and all these will end when death comes. It is God who offers us a happy eternal life through the sacrifice and death of His beloved Son, Jesus. Read John 3:16. I *pray* that we shall all meet again on that Great Day and that not one of my family shall be missing.

The following page contains my wishes on how the remaining things should be cared for.

Your loving mother, (signed) Mrs. Bertha E. Kuehnl

(My wish, Executor 1, George Kuehnl; Executor 2, Robert Kuehnl)

(Her second page noted her house paid for and equally to be distributed, bank accounts, gift to the church, policies, cemetery lots, personal things (Ruth C. Lampe diamond ring and sewing machine, which I have always treasured, and I gave Beth her ring because she loved Grammie so much, and Grammie loved her as she did all her grandchildren.)

She ended it. From all money received, please hold out $500 for each grandchild to be used as a wedding gift from Grandpa and Grammie Kuehnl.

She signed it. "Be Happy." Mom

A life well lived by Ruth Kuehnl Lampe—2012

It was my intent to tell a little about our own dear children and their families, but they preferred that I not and stop the story here, and so I honor their decision.

So I end this story in remembrance of so many things and so much worthwhile and good in my heart, and Mom, "we are happy." Thank you for that.

"The story we're called to tell and live and die by is one of risks confronted, death embraced. What's more, Jesus calls us to walk the narrow way, take up a cross with Him daily. It's terribly a risky business. Ask that bright company of martyrs that quite recklessly parted with goods, security, and life itself, preferring to be faithful in death rather than safe in life."

—William H. Willimon

To my darling Ruth

I'm in love with you. Always have been, always will be. I enjoy so very much being with you. Your strong Christian faith has been a bedrock for me. You always see good in every situation. Always optimistic, never pessimistic. When I have been weak, you have been very strong. During my long illness, you stood up for me when others would not believe. To me, this is true love. You have encouraged me through the years to become a better person, never dwelling on my failures. I know I wouldn't be alive today except for your strength and unfailing love. Your love is everywhere for me in our life together. As a wife, you fulfill all of my needs, bringing comfort and joy even in all the little things. Your love for people is powerful and an example for me and others. Jesus said, "The greatest of these is love." I pray that I am worthy and capable of receiving your love and expressing how very thankful I am.

Your partner, your husband,
who loves you always. Rol 2001

My Mother and Father soon after my
Dad came home at the end of WWI.

A Tribute to My Dear Husband, Rol

What perfect joy it was when first we met—
Laughter and joy and a wonder of love.
You were and always have been a romantic, which has meant
everything to me.
God planned it and walked with us, all the way.
You have always been supportive and made me feel so special in
your encouragement.
You always made me laugh with sweet, growing love that was
exciting and special to me.
Early in our marriage, coming in after a day of work,
Saying, "What can I do to lighten your load?" and that has never
changed.
There has never been a day that I have not seen you walking with
the Lord, in trials of your own or in caring about others. Such
a humble man.
You were found daily reading your Bible and living a gentle life
of respecting others and never getting angry or upset. I would
more than likely see your head bowed and talking to our Lord
than reacting in any way.
What God sees in you, Rol, is a wonderful man who is awilling
servant, an unselfish man, not without pain in your life, but
I believe God healed you because of your faithfulnessand
obedience.
Your role of father to your children and grandchildren has been
one of quiet acceptance and not judgment.
You have had faith in them and pray for them and don't offer
advice, unless asked.
A life well lived, and I am so proud to have been a part of it.
Thank you, dear Rol. Ours is an always love, and I thank you for it.

Your wife, always,
Ruth

AFTERWARD

(by Ruth C. Lampe)

This day, Jesus has lowered His net and has taken me in,

    I am sure of it.

From my earliest remembrances,

    He has led my path.

He gave me a family of love, but not without problems,

    So I could have endurance for things in life.

        I am sure of it.

He gave me a mother of quiet faith,

    That I never saw falter or stumble.

He gave me eyes to see that,

    This incredible faith that looked at life

        sweetly

            And with hope and assurance.

This was His gift to me,

    Her gift to me.

He gave me a father who cared,

    And showed love and respect for me.

The Lord guided my path,

    And gave me strengths that I pulled upon.

Jesus Christ, my Lord and my Savior, has guided me

    every step of the way,

        and how I felt that.

Growing up was easy,

    He protected me and, with love for others,

        guided me.

He showed me that others mattered in life,

    and that a life of faith and obedience

        was all He asked.

He gave me my precious husband

    who encouraged me and believed in me,

        and loved me, unconditionally,

        and faithfully.

He gave me our precious children,

    who have made life brighter, because of them.

He has given me our grandchildren,

    who I ask for guidance for, that

        they may find this

            well of life-giving hope

              I have found.

And He has given me friends,

    a joy in life that brings such comfort.

And He has given me Himself and has never,

    never let me down.

And now,

    I am ready for this "Afterward."

        And I thank you, Lord.

MY LIFE, MY HUSBAND

Rol and Ruth celebrating a wedding anniversary.

This is my dear husband, Rol Lampe, that continued to enrich my life in love and joy and direction to God. He knew the way, we met, and our journey continued on together.

Ruth Kuehnl Lampe

Ruth Lampe, author of *Life – Always a Choice of Doors* is proud to include in her book an article written by Michael C. Stockmaster, also of Toledo, Ohio. I love this article because it is all about the very City I grew up in and is related to many things in our family life during the Great Depression.

Tough Times in Toledo:
The WPA Rebuilds a City, 1935 to 1941
By Michael Stockmaster

On the eve of October 29, 1929, the day the New York Stock Exchange crashed, the people of Toledo, Ohio were little concerned about the economic future of their city.[1] Toledo, a booming, prosperous, and industrious town, had been growing in size and expanding economically throughout the late 19th and early 20th centuries. The city had grown to this point through large investments in industry and great leadership in business and government. Little did the people of Toledo know that their strongest points would also become their weakest ones and even their downfall over the next year, causing them to be one of the worst hit cities affected by the Great Depression. Many attempts to bring Toledo out of the Depression failed miserably and by 1932 its citizens could not see an end in sight. The current President, Herbert Hoover, unable to help the American people pull out of this Depression, was easily defeated in the election of 1932 by a more promising candidate, Franklin Delano Roosevelt. Fulfilling his promise of bringing the nation out of the Depression, Roosevelt created an alphabet soup of public assistance programs called the New Deal. Beginning in 1935, one of FDR's programs called the Works Progress Administration (WPA) came to Toledo and began assisting the unemployed and bringing the city back to the greatness it knew before the Depression.

Although founded and built on swampland, Toledo became an incorporated city in Northwest Ohio in the early 1830s and began its growth to greatness throughout the 19th and early 20th centuries. This greatness can be attributed to many reasons including a strong business and industrial base as well as great business and political leadership throughout the city. Because of this, many people immigrated to Toledo from all over the world, ready to work hard and looking for better living conditions compared to where they had come from before. Toledo was soon a cultural melting pot of many groups and ethnicities.

The essential reason Toledo's business and industrial base grew so quickly was due to the growth and development of transportation, commerce, and manufacturing. All three worked hand in hand to make Toledo a thriving city. The first important development was the transportation industry. It started out with the canal system in the mid 19th century. The Erie and Wabash Canal would help create a basic import and export system that would only develop more over time. The next major step in transportation brought the addition of railroads into the city's infrastructure. Toledo began developing its railway system in the latter half of the 19th century, and by the early 20th century, it had become a major railroad hub for the Midwest. Toledo connected the railroad lines east and west from New York out to Indiana and Illinois and north and south from Detroit to Cincinnati, thus even further developing the commerce coming in and going out of Toledo. The next transportation development that came along was the highway and street system in Toledo. These streets and highways were well thought out and developed to help traffic flow better within and out of the city. As early as 1862, Toledo began running horse- drawn streetcars to get people around the city, and eventually with the growth and development of the electric cable car and motor vehicles in the early 20th century, Toledo had a well-developed transportation network. At the same time, the city also continued on the path of improving its water transportation with the development of the Port of Toledo. While the early canal system had become obsolete, the use of the Maumee River as a port out to the Great Lakes was a major boost for commerce.[2]

Another major development in the growth of the city of Toledo was the increase in commerce and trade thanks to the transportation system. Trade in the early 20th century became one of the most important facets to the development of the city. Toledo was not only setup to help facilitate the transportation system but also to help with the commerce system by getting raw materials in and getting staples and manufactured goods out to the world. The major items that made commerce big in Toledo were grains that came from the surrounding farms and were stored in elevators at the Port of Toledo, food, dry goods, hardware, shoes, and other items that were made in the city and were transported around the country wherever they were needed.[3]

These items show that Toledo had the large and continually growing manufacturing and industrial base built up in the 19th and 20th centuries. Manufacturing developed along with the transportation and trade commerce in Toledo. The major manufacturing fronts in Toledo included the automotive industry, metals and machinery production, glass manufacturing, and petroleum refining. Many people were needed in the city to fill the demand for workers in factory jobs which brought in many different types of people from all around the world who were looking for a better life. These industries were the major backbone of Toledo's economic standing and would bring Toledo to greatness, but would also lead to its unfortunate fall during the Great Depression.[4]

Two of the first industries to move into Toledo were the Toledo Brewing and Malting Company in the 1850s and the Milburn Wagon Works in 1875 which made wagons through a completely mechanized production. The Wagon Works was the first real factory in Toledo. Another major industry that came in the latter half for the 19th century and helped establish Toledo as the "Glass Capital of the World" was the Libbey Glass factory in 1888. Eventually around 1900, two more glass entrepreneurs, Michael J. Owens and Edward Ford, moved into the Toledo area and joined up with Libbey. Together they expanded the glass industry to make Toledo the largest glass producer to date. Another industry that came and developed in Toledo around 1900 was the bicycle industry. The city of Toledo was home to at least ten different bicycle companies during this time and the industry brought many people to work in the factories from around the world. Due to the growing demand for refined oil during this time period, oil companies such as the National Supply Company, Craig Oil Company, and Sun Oil Company began refining oil in Toledo. The Acme Sucker Rod Company was also established at this time, producing an important mechanism for pulling the oil up from deep within the ground. From 1900 to 1915, one of the most important industries that came to Toledo was automobiles. John N. Willys started his company by buying out the Overland Automobile Company of Indianapolis, Indiana in 1907 and the Pope Motor Car Company in 1909, and creating the Willys-Overland Company. Willys then bought out the other companies that created the parts needed to make his cars and combined them under one company. Because of this move, Willys- Overland became the second largest producer of automobiles in the early 20th century.[5]

During World War I, Toledo was very helpful in the war because of its industry. The United States government came in and took over the factories within the city to help with the war effort. Companies such as Willys-Overland and Toledo Steel Products produced goods for the war such as airplanes, motors, and munitions while other companies such as the Ohio Canvas Goods Company and the M.I. Wilcox Company made tents and other canvas goods for the country. Toledo boomed from the need and production of goods for the war and many companies prospered from the additional workload.[6]

Toledo's prosperity was not only due to its industrial economy but also because of its great leadership, not only in the industry, but also in government. People like Edward Drummond Libbey and John N. Willys brought large industries into Toledo and helped revolutionize the ways that factories were run and made the city a better place in which to live and work. The great political leaders of this time included Samuel "Golden Rule" Jones and Brand Whitlock. Jones, the owner of the Acme Sucker Rod Company, decided to take on the corrupt city politics of his day and was elected mayor of Toledo for four consecutive terms. Known as one of the nation's top Progressives, Jones brought to the city better respect for the working class along with social reforms for the workers to make factory life a little easier on the common man. His social reforms also brought in free schools, parks, and a nonpartisan government. When Jones died in 1904, his friend Brand Whitlock continued on with Jones' progressive reforms. The combined efforts of these men made Toledo one of the best cities to live in and more and more people and industries poured in.[7]

Because of the fast growth of industry, Toledo had a high demand for more and more workers to run transportation, commerce, and the many factories in the city. This demand brought immigrants from all over the world to come make a better life in Toledo. From the beginning with the digging of the canals, Irish immigrants came for the work and to get away from the problems in their own country. Then came the Germans, the Polish, the Russians, and the Hungarians to help build and expand the city and its massive industrial base. Many people came from the tiny Kingdom of Bohemia in the Austro-Hungarian Empire. This was one of the most important glass producing regions in Europe. The Bohemians, today known as Czechs, found work in Toledo's growing glass industry. Each group came in waves to make a better place for their families in Toledo. When Toledo became an incorporated city in the 1830s, the population was just around 2000 people, while in just 100 years by 1930 the population had grown to almost 300,000 people.[8] Life up until about 1930 was looking pretty good for people in Toledo. A sign on top of the Valentine Theater in downtown Toledo put it this way - "You Will Do Better in Toledo." Little did the people of Toledo know what was going to happen on October 29, 1929 and how badly it would affect them.

On October 29, 1929, prices on the New York Stock Exchange came crashing down and millions lost all of their money in the bank failure and the panic that ensued. The Stock Market in the early 1920s had the biggest boom in its history to date with people investing more and more money in the system each year. But by September and October of 1929, the big boom was over. The market took a drastic hit and people began losing money fast. Banks closed and many businesses failed. Because of this, many people were laid off all at once. The job loss, the failing market, and the incapability of the government to put a quick fix on it sent the nation into the Great Depression of the 1930s. Herbert Hoover, the President at the time, felt that the economy would slowly correct itself. This "laissez faire" type of reaction by the President only hurt the economy even more by the early 1930s.[9]

Ohio was hit extremely hard by the Great Depression due to the industrial base at the heart of the state's economy. Overall by 1932, Ohio's unemployment rate was at an all time high of 37.7 percent. At its highest rate, Toledo industry suffered the worst out of all cities in Ohio with an unemployment rate of almost 80 percent.[10] This happened because Toledo's economy was intertwined with industry. Virtually the entire infrastructure of Toledo had something to do with industrial production. Transportation and commerce failed because there was nothing coming out of the factories.

he people who did not lose their jobs took heavy wage and hourly cuts and could barely survive on what they were making.

Although the Depression was in full swing, Toledo had plans for building projects already in the works to try and help with the massive unemployment in the city. Some of these projects included new construction at the University of Toledo, the completion of Our Lady Queen of the Most Holy Rosary Cathedral, and building the Ohio Savings Bank and Trust Company, which closed down within a year of its completion. Thanks to the Libbey Trust, the Toledo Museum of Art also added two additions onto the museum. But eventually these projects were completed and money ran out causing more and more problems for the once great city of Toledo.[11]

These were extremely tough times for Toledoans. Many families fell apart because they could not afford to stay together. Others just abandoned their homes to go out and look for any work they could find. Children stopped going to school so that they could look for work, just to earn pennies a day to try and help out their families. Many people would stand in bread lines waiting for anything they could get to help feed their families, and were often disappointed when the food ran out and they had to return home empty handed. Because many could not afford the mortgages or rent for their homes, they were foreclosed on and "Hoovervilles" began to pop up around Toledo as a place for displaced works and their families to live.12 Crime was also increasing in the city; people could not afford to pay for things anymore, so they just attempted to steal them. Few cared if they got caught because at least in jail they would get some food. A few headlines from the Toledo newspapers illustrate this:

Girls shot stealing food for children. Pleaded Guilty. Freed. 3000 Farmers gather for Crozier Auctions. Idle men form Barter League [13]

The Hoover Administration's lack of action to help bring the nation out of the Depression put a heavy burden on the states. In 1931, the State of

Ohio under the control of Democratic Governor George White, along with the state legislature, came up with ideas and an emergency plan of action to bring aid and relief to Ohioans. They began implementing programs that would create jobs in areas that would help reduce the unemployment rate but also help the state build up for the future. But in the end, these jobs, such as working on highway maintenance and collecting and distributing clothes for the Red Cross, were only a small help, and would not be a major factor in regaining control over the toppling economy of the state. Across the nation, states as well as cities began demanding that the federal government step in, and offer some sort of aid to help bring everyone out of the Depression or the nation would fall even farther into disaster.[14]

Due to the massive failure to help bring the nation out of the Depression, the Hoover administration was hated by the unemployed, devastated, and angry American people. They needed someone to bring change and relief to the United States. This change came in the Presidential Election of 1932, which ushered Franklin Delano Roosevelt into the White House as the 32nd President of the United States of America. Roosevelt ran as a Democrat on the promise of a "New Deal" for America which would bring the change needed to help end the Great Depression and recover the nation as a whole. Because of the hatred for Hoover and the Republican Party, FDR won by an outstanding margin throughout the nation. In Ohio alone, he won by almost 74,000 votes. To help FDR, the Democratic Party also took the majority in the House and Senate, making it very easy to pass new legislation to help get the nation back on its feet.[15]

Roosevelt's New Deal legislation would be the key to help aid and bring relief to people all over America and especially to the citizens of Toledo. As soon as Roosevelt was sworn into office, he began the most difficult job of bringing the nation out of the Depression. His first task under the New Deal was to stabilize the banking system. To do this, he ordered a

"Bank Holiday". All of the nation's banks were closed temporarily. This stopped "runs" on the banks by the frightened depositors. It gave the government time to loan money to the banks so they could reopen. Just as importantly during his first term as President, he started what many called an "alphabet soup" of government relief and aid programs to "pump prime" the nation's struggling economy. Some of the most important ones included the Federal Emergency Relief Administration (FERA), the Civil Works Administration (CWA), the Public Works Administration (PWA), the Agricultural Adjustment Administration (AAA), the National Industrial Recovery Act (NIRA), and the Civilian Conservation Corps (CCC). Programs such as these brought relief money and jobs to Ohio through the creation of various projects to get people working again and states like Ohio moving in the right direction.

Most specifically for Ohio, programs like the NIRA and the AAA brought aid to the industrial factories and farmers within the state. They helped stimulate the economy and were thus very helpful to the city of Toledo. The NIRA was setup to help recover the industrial base that had been lost, especially in Ohio. The first part the plan was to allow businesses to start regulating themselves and to bring fair trade to encourage more effective and less cut-throat competition. This program also gave the workers the right to organize and form labor unions, which would help bring fairer wages and better working conditions to factories throughout Ohio and the rest of the nation. This act, along with the Wagner-Connery Act which was passed later in 1935 when the NIRA was found unconstitutional, would bring about the labor unions in modern American society. Toledo was one of the first places in Ohio to exercise the rights of laboring people to organize when in the spring of 1934, workers at the Electric Auto-Lite factory struck to get better conditions. Sadly, the strike ended violently and few of the union's concessions were met. The AAA was also an important program for Ohio. Ohio farmers who participated in this program reduced the number of crops and livestock they produced for market in exchange for money from the government. This increased the price of the crops and livestock because there was less supply in the market but still the same demand.[16] Farmers also received loans from the government to help them pay their mortgages.

These programs created by the Roosevelt Administration's "First New Deal" began to help rebuild the nation, but were not enough to bring the nation out of the troubles into which it had fallen. With unemployment still at an extremely high rate and consumer confidence at an all time low, Roosevelt knew he needed to bring more aid and help to get the nation back on its feet. He began implementing more aid programs in 1935 calling them his "Second New Deal." The "Second New Deal" was geared more towards ending the current depression and preventing it from happening again as well as aiding the American worker more directly. During this time, there were many new programs that helped the ailing rural farmers. The Resettlement Administration moved farmers off of their old farms that were not producing crops and onto new, more fertile lands. After the farmers were moved, the government came in and began repairing and replenishing the nutrients in the previously unusable soil so that more farmers could come in and replant. The Resettlement Administration helped to construct two low cost housing communities in Ohio to help relieve the people that were displaced from their farms.[17]

The Soil Conservation and Domestic Allotment Act of 1936 gave money to farmers to switch from growing crops such as tobacco, which destroyed the soil, to crops that would make the soil more nutrient enriched so they could grow more and also help prevent erosion, which was a major problem in the Great Plains region with the Dust Bowl. Farmers everywhere, including Ohio, also benefited from the Rural Electrification

Act (REA), which not only brought electricity out to the rural farms and towns, but also created more jobs to do the work of getting it out there.[18]

Although many of the "Second New Deal" programs dealt with the rebuilding of the rural farms, Roosevelt also included programs that would help the average American for the future. One program that was established during this time was the Federal Housing Administration (FHA). This program was setup to help get money and loans for low income families so they could buy or build houses. It also brought in federal grant money to help improve housing and clear out slums in the cities. The cities of Cleveland and Cincinnati were some of the first in the nation to obtain money from the FHA to help during this time.[19] Another program for the future that was started by the Roosevelt Administration was the creation of the Social Security Act in 1935. This act started the collection out of the people's wages that would be given back to them after retirement. This became very helpful to the elderly people who after retirement had little to no money to survive on, and to people who could not work such as the disabled and blind, especially during the Depression. The Social Security Act is the longest lasting program in Roosevelt's New Deal and is still active to this day.[20]

Out of all of Roosevelt's New Deal programs the one that was most important to Ohio, especially to Toledo, was the Works Progress Administration (WPA). The WPA was the answer to many Toledoans' prayers for relief from the Depression. The WPA, like many of the other works programs created previously, would bring relief through funding building projects which created much needed jobs in Toledo. This program, however, would far surpass any of the expectations of the previous programs. The WPA created and completed the most projects of any other program that came to Toledo, and would be the most helpful in returning Toledo back to a great and prosperous city.

With the failure and collapse of the FERA program, the president enacted the Emergency Relief Appropriation Act of 1935 which would bring funding and assistance to needy Americans through work on federal public projects instead of just government handouts. This was important because it made the average unemployed American feel as if he or she was doing something to earn money instead of sitting back and collecting relief funds. The WPA was created from this act on May 6, 1935 and was up and running by July under the control of Harry L. Hopkins, the former Administrator of FERA. The WPA was a very well thought out and organized relief program. To start a new project, a sponsor who would be asking for the WPA's help, would bring the project in to the local WPA administration and go through an approval process. Once approved at the local level, it would be taken to the state office for approval, and then on to the national level. Once the project was approved, it would go on for planning and then starting of the project. The WPA in Ohio, run by Dr. Carl Watson, was broken down into four divisions to make the program run smoothly and effectively. First, the Operations Division took care of approval and planning of all of the construction and building projects, as well as making sure they were inspected and completed. The non-construction projects were controlled and completed by the Division of Women's and Professional projects. The Division of Employment would handle finding the people to work on the projects as well watching over labor, wages, and complaints. The final group was the Division of Finance which controlled the payroll, the money spent on projects, and timekeeping. This administrative organization helped the WPA run smoothly and get projects done quickly and efficiently.[21]

The next step for getting a WPA project started was to obtain the funding. Most of the money for the labor and supervision for the projects was provided through the WPA and the money set aside by the Emergency

Relief Appropriation Act of 1935. The money to obtain materials, equipment, and supplies was split up between the government and the local sponsoring group of the project. In most cases, depending on the size of the project, the WPA would provide about 80% of the funds, while the sponsoring group would provide the other 20%.[22] The sponsors were also required to do most of the ground work for the projects including estimating total costs, how much labor would be needed, providing supervisory staff over the project, and the purchasing of the land needed for the project.[23] Most of the money was given to the people working on the projects as wages for their work. Eighty six out of every 100 dollars went towards the cost of labor on most WPA projects in Toledo. To save money on supplies for new buildings and projects, the city of Toledo demolished and salvaged materials from old, abandoned buildings such as the Milburn Wagon Works, the Lucas County Armory, the Wabash Elevator, and St. Mary's Church. Other later programs, such as the Public Works Administration (PWA), also gave grants and loans to the sponsoring groups to help pay for the costs of labor and materials.[24] Finding funding for these projects was not always an easy task. Many projects stalled or failed because of the lack of funds or interest in the project. Even with these problems, from the beginning of the WPA in Ohio in 1935 to its highest peak in 1938, the United States Government and the project sponsors provided the state nearly a half a billion dollars to help rebuild and recover from the Depression.[25]

Ohio received a great amount of aid from the WPA, making it one of the best places to find a job. The reasons Ohio was such a popular place for the WPA was because of the high unemployment rate and for political reasons. The large industrial infrastructure that had made Ohio boom in the early 20th century led to an extremely large unemployment rate when the factories shut down. Hundreds of thousands of people were unemployed and needed something to get them back on their feet. Another reason Ohio did so well in obtaining WPA projects was because of politics. Roosevelt, a Democrat, knew that the election would soon be on him again, and that Ohio was a swing state. To gain favor, he would make sure that projects and jobs would go out to Ohio. The aid and relief helped Roosevelt win the 1936 election by a landslide in Ohio and other states across the nation.[26]

The city of Toledo was in the top four cites in Ohio for government aid and relief through the WPA because of the need for jobs and to continue the expansion of the city. . When the projects began coming in, people were excited to get back to work. To work for the WPA, you would be chosen by a relief agency as a person who was in need of assistance money. The WPA was required to have 95% of their workforce selected from this group, but they would be able to hand pick the supervisory staff to oversee the project. People were also selected by their occupational status. The white collar worker would stick with white collar jobs and the blue collar people would work the blue collar jobs. This was important because it helped reduce the number of unskilled workers on the projects, which in the end would make the projects run more smoothly. Wages for the workers varied depending on the size of the city and whether or not it was a skilled or unskilled job. The pay scale ranged from $45 to $95 a month depending on what you were doing. Although it did not sound like much, this money would help provide relief to thousands all over Toledo.[27] By September 1935, Ohio had twelve counties that had more than 25 percent of the families with at least one family member working for the WPA. Also in that year, Ohio had the largest number of people employed, besides Pennsylvania, on the WPA payroll with about 287,000.[28]

When the Works Progress Administration came to Toledo, Ohio in 1935, the city was in terrible financial trouble. City and state-wide relief had run out and many projects started by other New Deal programs slowed or came to a halt in the middle of the projects. These failed projects soon became the responsibility of the WPA in Toledo. Projects such as Canal Boulevard, later renamed the Anthony Wayne Trail, a new parking lot for the zoo, the Naval Armory, and the William W. Roche Tuberculosis Hospital were started by earlier programs and finished by the WPA. From 1935 to 1941, the WPA created and started many projects throughout Toledo to help rebuild. Some of the major projects included new buildings and major repair at the Toledo Zoo and the Toledo Metroparks, the Toledo Public Schools, and the University of Toledo. Other smaller construction projects were completed as well, including streets and roads, water and sewer projects, and flood control projects. There were also many WPA sponsored projects that did not involve construction including public, health, and educational services. One of the least known projects included in the WPA was a cultural program called Federal Project One.

Possibly the most noticeable projects put on by the WPA in Toledo were the buildings at the Toledo Zoo. Along with the additions of the Canal Boulevard and the new parking lot, the zoo also continued projects started by previous programs and started new construction projects on several buildings and exhibits throughout the zoo. These buildings include the Reptile House, Monkey Mountain, the Museum of Science, which included the Indoor Theater and Outdoor Amphitheater, the Aviary, the Aquarium, the Conservatory, and the underground pedestrian tunnel. The projects began as early as 1935 and continued through 1939, employing thousands of workers from Toledo, and giving them the satisfaction of a paying job. Many of the buildings at the zoo were designed with Spanish influences in architecture, in keeping with the city's name, and due to the high cost of materials, most were made from recycled buildings from around the city. Many of these buildings and projects still survive at the Toledo Zoo today making it one of the best and most historic zoos in the nation.[29]

Another location around Toledo that benefited from the WPA projects and funds was the local Toledo Metroparks and the other local parks. The WPA, along with the CCC, took on projects at the Metroparks which included creating walking and biking paths, shelter houses, athletic fields, roads, and landscaping. Other projects at the Metroparks included repairing the lift locks at Side Cut Park along with ten dams and six bridges at Pearson Park. Getting some help from Toledo businessmen, WPA work and funds were also instrumental in the acquisition and creation of Oak Openings Park, a $375,000 project in 1938. By the end of 1938, over 1,400 men were employed by the Toledo Metroparks.30 City parks also benefited from the WPA projects including work at over ten parks. Projects that were included in just the first two years of the WPA included a swimming pool and bath house at Scott Park, three shelter houses, 40 tennis courts, 38 horseshoe courts, 32 baseball diamonds, nine bridges, two skating rinks, and the Ottawa Park amphitheater.[31]

The University of Toledo also joined in on the WPA projects and funds. Beginning in 1935, the university obtained funding from federal and local sponsors for over $330,000 to begin the building of the Glass Bowl football stadium. This building, with very few changes and additions completed to it, is still currently used University of Toledo Rockets football. A baseball field and eight tennis courts were also added by the WPA to the University of Toledo Campus. By bringing jobs and relief to many Toledoans, the WPA helped establish the University of Toledo as one of the premier universities in Ohio.[32]

The WPA also completed many projects on the public schools around Toledo. As many as 45 schools were painted by the WPA and seven others had extensive and much needed repairs done on them. Other schools, such as Beverly, Newberry, and Woodward High School, were enlarged and improved including additions of larger gyms. The repair of the grounds at Libbey High School and the building of a new stadium at Waite High

School also helped provide jobs to unemployed Toledoans. Overall, the WPA brought in over $635,000 for the much needed repairs for the city schools. Many of the historic WPA school repairs can still be seen throughout Toledo today.[33]

With the constantly increasing population in Toledo, the need for more public libraries increased. Because of this, on September 4, 1940, the Toledo Public Library opened its new building at the corner of Michigan and Madison in Downtown Toledo at the site of the old Toledo High School. The library, funded primarily by the PWA and constructed by WPA workers, featured glass murals that were created by the Libbey-Owens-Ford Glass Company. With a cost of nearly 2 million dollars, the Main Branch Library brought work to many Toledo workers and continues to be one the best public libraries in the nation.[34]

The city of Toledo also benefited from other WPA projects. All around Toledo, improvements and much needed repairs were being completed. Over 330 miles of city streets and county roads were improved, including 100 dirt roads being paved into smooth highways, and repairing more than 200 brick city streets repaired. Another improvement project was the addition and repair of thirty-five miles of storm sewers throughout the city and the addition of seven miles of water lines, giving 50 men a total of 22 months of work. Thousands of Toledoans were also employed to work on flood control, which included cleaning, widening, straightening and deepening over a thousand miles of ditches and creeks to help prevent floods, sewer conditions, and mosquito breeding. The projects and repairs overall cost well over 10 million dollars, paid out by the WPA and local sponsors, and brought some much needed repair and thousands of jobs to the city.[35]

Although many of the projects put on by the WPA were construction projects, important public service projects were also funded. These non-construction projects included projects in the Division of Women's and Professional. Education and schools were a very important part of this group of programs. Some projects included the cooking of school lunches and the hiring of many unemployed teachers to help educate thousands of adult Toledoans who had never finished school through the Federal Adult Education program.[36] Another important public project put on by the WPA was a health program. The health project included running clinics to help the people who could not afford medical checkups when they got sick and getting children tested and immunized for diseases such as tuberculosis and diphtheria. With all of the construction jobs going to the men, many women also were also given jobs funded by the WPA. These projects not only helped provide jobs for the working women, but also helped out by providing a service to the people of Toledo. Sewing projects, which included the production of 20,000 rugs and almost a million garments, helped out the needy people of Toledo. Also included in the sewing projects was the repair and creation of over 700,000 toys for children at Christmas time, who most likely would not have received any gifts because of the lack of money in the family. The public library and schools also benefited from the public works with the mending and rebinding of over 300,000 books.[37]

One of the least known projects of the Works Progress Administration was a cultural program called Federal Project One. This project created work for people who did not work in construction, but still needed work including artists, musicians, actors, and writers. Federal Project One was created in the fall of 1935, and created jobs for over 40,000 workers nationwide, including over 1,500 in Ohio. The Federal Art projects, which employed about 155 people in Ohio, included painters, photographers, mural designers, ceramics modelers, and lithographers.

These artists, through there work, provided community improvements as well as decoration for many buildings across the state. Paul Breisach, a

Toledo artist, was hired by this project and began painting historic murals of Admiral Oliver Hazard Perry's Lake Erie victory in the War of 1812 for the new Naval Armory. Other art projects in Toledo included the creation of a cinematic pictorial history of the WPA in Toledo, the creation of safety films for the Board of Education, and a puppet show, which presented ideas on safety and morality. Also included in the Arts Project was the Toledo Zoo, which received funds for creating more natural habitats for animals and better displays for the Natural History Museum. [38]

Another program created under Federal Project One was the Federal Music Project. The music project was created for not only musical entertainment but also music education. Over 2,000 programs were put on by the music project between December 1935 and July 1936, bringing in over 864,000 people in to hear. Funding for musical groups and orchestras was given to cities all over Ohio, including Toledo. The Toledo Orchestra put on many great free concerts at the Civic Auditorium and the newly constructed Toledo Zoo Amphitheater. The Toledo's Orchestra was widely popular and well respected for its work and given great reviews by newspapers, citizens, and even First Lady Eleanor Roosevelt on a visit to Toledo. Also added by the Federal Music project was the celebration of National Music Week which included moreconcerts and music education for the people of Ohio.[39]

In Ohio, the Federal Theater project employed 187 workers, who produced and acted in more than 25 plays and many vaudeville and variety shows throughout the state. Some of the shows put on by the Toledo Federal Theater included Hatcher Hughes' Hell Bent for Heaven, Thomas Buchanan's A Woman's Way and Mis' Nellie of N'Orleans, and Edgar Wallace's Criminal at Large. The Toledo projects were sponsored by the local Toledo Repertoire Company and provided its theater and equipment for the plays. Many Toledoans went to these shows to escape from the everyday life that the Depression was putting on them and they became largely popular. [40]

The final part of Federal Project One is the Federal Writers Project, which started with two main projects, The Ohio Guide and the survey of state and local historical records. The Ohio Guide, started on November 1, 1935 was a state wide project in which 350 writers began working on a comprehensive guide for Ohioans and tourists to Ohio. The Ohio Guide was an addition to the six volume American Guide for the entire nation. In this guide, the writer would provide information over historical and geographical knowledge of Ohio as well as the greater part of the book, dealing with folk lore, ethnology, points of interest, churches, clubs, tours, accommodations, and transportation facilities. This 800 page guide would provide illustrations and maps of places all over Ohio. The other part of the Writers Project included the Historical Records Survey. This project was setup to preserve and make accessible the history of Ohio and other states. Many historical records at this time did not seem very important to anyone, but with the creation of the program, much history was saved. Many historical records had been destroyed over the years or left in piles in an attic to collect dust and rot. The workers on this project would go in and restore or write down this information and store it logically for the future, providing historians, sociologists, and political scientists information for future writing projects. [41]

Although a sometimes forgotten program of the WPA, the Federal Project One was very important to help the United States come out of the Great Depression. This project not only generated thousands of jobs and training opportunities across Ohio, but it also created and preserved many works of value, and created a better appreciation for the arts. Without this project of the WPA, the arts, in general, and historical knowledge would not be the same as they are today.

The Works Progress Administration created an everlasting legacy in the history of Toledo. During the Depression, the WPA was the most effective of Franklin D. Roosevelt's "New Deal" programs for Toledo. Although no final tally of projects in Ohio was ever put together, the WPA created many projects and jobs for the needy and unemployed Ohioans. The city of Toledo benefited from the projects that can still be seen today, including those at the Toledo Zoo, the Metroparks, and The University of Toledo, to all of the social and cultural projects that were created from 1935 to 1941. The City of Toledo took all of the help they possibly could from the WPA to help bring them back to the great city they were before the Great Depression.

Even with the help of the WPA, Toledo still had not risen completely out of the Great Depression. In the late 1930s, the powerful German leader, Adolf Hitler began his war against Poland and the Allied Powers of Great Britain and France in turn declared war on him. The United States, which did not want to be involved in another world war, in the beginning stayed neutral to the war, but eventually started sending aid to the allied powers. This aid began to switch the United States from a peace time economy to a war time economy. With the last straw being dropped on December 7, 1941 at the bombing of Pearl Harbor by the Japanese, the United States joined the Allied Forces in World War II. Although the WPA helped to stimulate the ailing Toledo economy, WWII was what really brought the city fully out of the Depression. The war time economy was booming for the previously failed industries and factories as Toledo became a major city in creating a national defense. Factories all over Toledo began to open up and produce items needed for the war. The Willys-Overland Factory began production on light armored cars, and shells and casings. The once high unemployment rate dropped quickly as more and more war time goods were needed.42 As more and more men were needed for factory work and eventually to go and fight in the war, the WPA rolls were reduced very quickly and by 1941, almost all the WPA programs were shut down. The WPA, although not the primary end of the Great Depression, helped Toledo rebuild into the great and prosperous city it once was. Many of the projects created by the WPA still stand today and are an important part of the history of the people and the City of Toledo.

Endnotes

[1]   Tana Mosier Porter, *Toledo Profile: A Sesquicentennial History* (Toledo: Toledo-Lucas County Public Library, 1987), 81.

[2]   Albert George Ballert, *The Primary Functions of Toledo,* Ohio (Chicago: The University of Chicago, 1947), 45- 100.

[3]   Ibid., 113-151.

[4]   Ibid., 152-196.

[5]   Porter, *Toledo Profile*, 53-57, 62-63.

[6]   Ibid., 69.

[7]   Ibid, 65-66.

[8]   Ibid., 75.

[9]   "Great Depression," *Ohio History Central*, accessed 1 March 2009, available from http://www.ohiohistorycentral.org/entry.php?rec=500; internet.

[10] George W. Knepper, *Ohio and Its People* (Kent, Ohio: The Kent State University, 2003), 354.

[11] Porter, *Toledo Profile*, 82-85.

[12] Jack K. Paquette, *A Boy's Journey Through the Great Depression* (No City Given: Xlibris Corporation, 2005), 21.

[13] Carl Wittk, *The History of the State of Ohio: Volume VI Ohio in the Twentieth Century 1900-1938* (Columbus: The Ohio State Archaeological and Historical Society, 1942), 438.

[14] Ibid., 439-440.

[15] Knepper, *Ohio and Its People*, 359.

[16] Ibid., 359-364.

[17] Wittke, *History of the State of Ohio*, 471-472.

[18] Knepper, *Ohio and Its People*, 359.

[19] Ibid., 355.

[20] "Social Security Act," *Ohio History Central, accessed 1 March 2009*, available from http://www.ohiohistorycentral.org/entry.php?rec=1433;internet.

[21] Wittke, *History of the State of Ohio*, 462.

[22] Ibid., 463.

[23] Richard D. Dorn, *A New Deal for the Glass City: Local Initiatives for Federal Aid During the Great Depression in Toledo, Ohio* (Toledo, Ohio: The University of Toledo, 1992), 151.

[24] Porter, *Toledo Profile*, 86-87.

[25] Wittke, *History of the State of Ohio*, 466.

[26] Knepper, *Ohio and Its People*, 361.

[27] Wittke, *History of the State of Ohio*, 462-464.

[28] Knepper, *Ohio and Its People*, 360.

[29] Ted Ligibel, *The Toledo Zoo's First 100 Years: A Century of Adventure* (Virginia Beach, Virginia: The Donning Company/Publishers, 1999), 47-60.

[30] Porter, *Toledo Profile*, 86.

[31] Lowell Nussbaum, "Only 2 Years Old But What a Baby!," *Toledo News Bee* 5 July 1937.

32 Ibid., 86.

33 Ibid., 86.

34 Ibid., 87-92

35 Nussbaum, "Only 2 Years Old."

36 Ibid.; Wittke, *History of the State of Ohio*, 467.

37 Nussbaum, "Only 2 Years Old."

38 United States, *Federal Project One [Cultural program of the] W.P.A. in Ohio. Art-music-theater-writers- historical records* (Columbus, Ohio: Works Progress Administration, 1936), 9-12.

39 United States, *Federal Project One,* 15-21.

40 Ibid., 25-29.

41 Ibid., 32-45.

42 Porter, *Toledo Profile*, 98.

List of Sources Primary Sources

Nussbaum, Lowell. "Only 2 Years Old But What a Baby!," *Toledo News Bee* 5 July 1937.

Paquette, Jack K. *A Boys Journey through the Great Depression*. No City Given: Xlibris Corp, 2005.

Searles, Clair K. & Moore, Franklin G. *Distribution of Federal Work Relief Programs in Lucas County: 1933-1937*. Toledo, OH: University of Toledo, 1 April 1938.

United States. Works Progress Administration. Ohio, *Federal Project One [Cultural program of the] W.P.A. in Ohio*. Art-music-theater-writers-historical records. :1936.

Secondary Sources

Dorn, Richard D. *A New Deal for the Glass City: Local Initiatives for Federal Aid During the Great Depression in Toledo, Ohio*. Toledo, Ohio: The University of Toledo, 1992.

"Great Depression", *Ohio History Central,* accessed 1 March 2009; available from http://www.ohiohistorycentral.org/entry.php?rec=500. July 1, 2005.; internet.

Knepper, George W. *Ohio and its People. Kent,* Ohio: The Kent State University Press, 2003. Ligibel, Ted. The Toledo Zoo's First 100 Years: a Century of Adventure. Virginia Beach, Virginia: The Donning Company/Publishers, 1999.

Mauk, Clint. *Historical Tales of Toledo*. Maumee, Ohio: Woodlands, 2004.

Messer-Kruse, Timothy. *Banksters, Bosses, and Smart Money: A Social History of the Great Toledo Bank Crash of 1931*. Columbus: Ohio State University Press, 2004.

Porter, Tana *M. Toledo Profile: A Sesquicentennial History*. Toledo, Ohio: Toledo-Lucas Country Public Library, 1987.

"Social Security Act," *Ohio History Central*, accessed 1 March 2009; available from http://www.ohiohistorycentral.org/entry.php?rec=1433. July 1, 2005; internet.

Sternsher, Bernard. "Depression and New Deal in Ohio: Lorena A. Hickok's Reports to Harry Hopkins, 1934-1936" *Ohio History: The Scholarly Journal of the Ohio State Historical Society.* V. 86, accessed 1 March 2009; available from http://www.ohiohistory.org; internet.

Wittke, Carl. *The History of State of Ohio: Volume VI Ohio in the Twentieth Century 1900-1938*. Columbus: The Ohio State Archaeological and Historical Society, 1942.

© *Michael Stockmaster, 2010*
Michael Stockmaster graduated from Lourdes College in May of 2009 with a BA in History.

Following is the authorization to use this material. Ruth Lampe

NOTE: I, Michael C Stockmaster, authorize Ruth Lampe to use my article *Tough Times in Toledo: The WPA Rebuilds a City, 1935 to 1941* in her book *Life - Always a Choice of Doors*. The article can be reprinted in her book in its entirety or parts as long as proper credit to me, the author, is being given. The article was completed and published on the Lourdes College Online Narrative History in 2010, but I own all of the rights to it.

Thank you Michael. I am proud to have this factual and very interesting account in my book. It brings the past back and we lived so much of it as a family. Ruth Lampe 2-13-13

REMEMBERING WITH PICTURES AND FACTS

FACTS

Our involvement/and much of the world's involvement in World War II: (this information was compiled by the BBC.uk and permission to use granted to author by Karen Pine On behalf of BBC News Website permission requests email 10/11/12)

I am using this timeline prepared from the United Kingdom's history—they were in this war a few years before the United States got involved through the attack of the Japanese on Pearl Harbor—it became our involvement then, also—I thought this preparation was necessary to show how our own nation was closely watching this war—our radio was on constantly when my dad was home not only because of what was happening in our world but because of how we then became involved—I was 9 years old when this started, barely getting out of our struggle during the Great Depression—I felt this timeline covered much of what the Allies did together and was more concise—Ruth Lampe, author

1 September 1939: Germany invades Poland

German forces attack Poland across all frontiers and its planes bomb Polish cities, including the capital, Warsaw—Britain and France prepare to declare war.

3 September 1939: Britain and France declare war on Germany

Britain and France are at war with Germany following the invasion of Poland two days ago.

10 May 1940: Churchill takes helm as Germans advance

German forces invade the Low Countries by air and land, while in London, Chamberlain is replaced by Churchill.

4 June 1940: Dunkirk rescue is over—Churchill defiant

As the last Allied soldier leaves Dunkirk, the British Prime Minister vows his forces "shall never surrender".

14 June 1940: German troops enter Paris

German troops march into Paris forcing French and allied troops to retreat.

World War II

10 Jul 1940	: Luftwaffe launches Battle of Britain
07 Sep 1940	: London blitzed by German bombers
15 Sep 1940	: Victory for RAF in Battle of Britain
15 Nov 1940	: Germans bomb Coventry to destruction
22 Jun 1941	: Hitler invades the Soviet Union
14 Aug 1941	: Secret meetings seal US-Britain alliance
07 Dec 1941	: Japanese planes bomb Pearl Harbor
11 Dec 1941	: Germany and Italy declare war on US
15 Feb 1942	: Singapore forced to surrender
15 Apr 1942	: Malta gets George Cross for bravery

07 Jun 1942	: Japanese beaten in Battle of Midway
19 Aug 1942	: Allies launch daring raid on Dieppe
04 Nov 1942	: Rommel goes on the run at El Alamein
01 Dec 1942	: Beveridge lays welfare foundations
17 Dec 1942	: Britain condemns massacre of Jews
02 Feb 1943	: Germans surrender at Stalingrad
16 May 1943	: Germans crush Jewish uprising
17 May 1943	: RAF raid smashes German dams
10 Jul 1943	: Western Allies invade Sicily
25 Jul 1943	: Italian dictator Mussolini quits
03 Sep 1943	: Allied troops invade mainland Italy
08 Sep 1943	: Italy's surrender announced
01 Dec 1943	: Allies united after Tehran conference
27 Jan 1944	: Leningrad siege ends after 900 days
18 May 1944	: Monte Cassino falls to the Allies
05 Jun 1944	: Celebrations as Rome is liberated
06 Jun 1944	: D-Day marks start of Europe invasion
20 Jul 1944	: Hitler survives assassination attempt
01 Aug 1944	: Uprising to free Warsaw begins
25 Aug 1944	: Paris is liberated as Germans surrender
17 Sep 1944	: Airborne invasion of Holland begins
26 Sep 1944	: Airborne troops retreat from Arnhem
03 Oct 1944	: Poles surrender after Warsaw uprising
17 Dec 1944	: Germany counter-attacks in Ardennes
27 Jan 1945	: Auschwitz death camp liberated
07 Feb 1945	: Black Sea talks plan defeat of Germany
14 Feb 1945	: Thousands of bombs destroy Dresden
23 Feb 1945	: US flag raised over Iwo Jima
15 Apr 1945	: British troops liberate Bergen-Belsen

21 Apr 1945	: Red Army enters outskirts of Berlin
27 Apr 1945	: Russians and Americans link at Elbe
28 Apr 1945	: Italian partisans kill Mussolini
01 May 1945	: Germany announces Hitler is dead
07 May 1945	: Germany signs unconditional surrender
08 May 1945	: Rejoicing at end of war in Europe
21 Jun 1945	: US troops take Okinawa
16 Jul 1945	: Allied leaders gather at Potsdam
26 Jul 1945	: Churchill loses general election
06 Aug 1945	: US drops atomic bomb on Hiroshima
09 Aug 1945	: Atom bomb hits Nagasaki
15 Aug 1945	: Allied nations celebrate VJ Day
02 Sep 1945	: Japan signs unconditional surrender
24 Oct 1945	: United Nations Organisation is born
20 Nov 1945	: Nuremberg trial of Nazis begins

My grandparents—
My father's father and his very loved step-mother

PICTURE OF GRANDFATHER KUEHNL'S
GROCERY STORE
45 CITY PARK AVE.
TOLEDO, OHIO

THE GROCERY STORE is something I remember a little as a small girl because we would go visit. We would all stand around in the store, we children along with our parents and waited patiently until Grandmother asked us to pick out a candy from this wonderful candy compartment. We also got to go in the back of the store, which was the home they lived in, and also upstairs when Grandmother was very ill. It was like something out of C.S. Lewis' Wardrobe story because it was so fascinating and such a thrill. We were very obedient children and were observant but never noisy. I loved the big kitchen with the wood burning stove to cook on.

My Father worked at the store till he left to join the Army just before WWI.

Mom and Dad's first home – 58 City Park

First house above is 38 City Park Avenue (Toledo, Ohio)—right across from the Grocery Store—the third one down with the awnings is 34 where my parents moved in December, 1923 (Dad built this home—and, after they moved to Glynn Court, Aunt Marie, Uncle Glenn, Carol and Marilyn bought the house and lived there. I recently talked to my cousin Carol Brown Lewellyn 7/29/2009 and she said that she was brought to their home right after she was born—as was her sister Marilyn who was 2-1/2 years younger—and they lived there till she was about 8 and then moved to Jackson, Michigan.) She told me that my Dad did build the house but she did not know that they lived there till they moved to Glynn Court. I, also, did not know that my parents lived there but when I was young, Aunt Marie and Uncle Glenn invited me for lunch with them (and it might have been an overnight, I cannot remember, but I remember very well sitting in the kitchen at the table with all of them having lunch). I also remember the dining room but not other parts of the house. I never dreamed that I was in the home that my Mother and Dad lived in from December, 1923 till moving to Glynn Court. Very special.

THIS IS A TIMELINE THAT I FIGURED OUT FROM MY MOTHER'S WRITTEN INFORMATION:

1) Dad's Mother Elize died when he was nine (she was 36 years old) in 1903. (childbirth)
2) Mom and Dad married 6/24/1920—they purchased a new home on 58 City Park—down the street from the family store.
3) My sister Violet was born and died in that house—at 58 City Park—August 24, 1921.
4) In Sept. 1923, Dad sold 58 City Park to Leopold Kornmueller (husband of Bertha, my Dad's sister)
5) Mom and Dad lived with them till December, 1923 till new house Dad was building at 34 City Park was finished.
6) Marie was born December 26, 1923 at 58 City Park—her Mother died in early February in Mom and Dad's new home at 34 City Park.
7) Marie's mother Bertha lived 6 weeks after Marie was born (kidney problem). On her deathbed, she asked if my Mother and Dad would take care of Marie because she was sickly (she was allergic to milk and still is).
8) Mom took care of Marie when her Mother was in the Hospital in January, 1924 and then she died in their home.
9) Mom and Dad raised Marie from 6 weeks to 11 months and then her Father took her back (he had other young children and Marie's mother had wisely thought it would be hard for him to take care of a sickly baby). She came back just a couple months before she was three and was with them all her growing up years. She assumed the name Kuehnl in grade school, per Mom, because it was confusing to live with us and have a different last name. Her Father never let them adopt her though. Ruth Kuehnl Lampe 7/29/09

'The Grocery Store'

My father's parents owned and ran this store and later Uncle Harold ran it for years.

When I was a little girl, most shopping was done at the grocery store. My father's parents ran a grocery store.

You went up to the counter with your grocery list and they filled your order as you waited. You had no comparative shopping in those days and you also didn't get choice cuts of meat because they wrapped what they wanted to. For the most part. When my mother sent me to the corner market she always said 'make sure you watch the butcher that he doesn't give you fatty meat or meat that didn't look good'. Did it work? I don't think so. (Not at the family grocery store, I am sure!) I was about 10 when A&P market opened close by and we had a family excursion there each Friday after dinner and we had a grocery cart that we were able to push and fill with what we wanted, with selections. Great Fun!

THIS WAS A PHONE OF THE 30'S AND 40'S.

Party lines for non-business subscribers were the rule before World War II, not the exception. In cities and country, most people shared a line with two to ten to twenty people. You could talk only five minutes or so before someone else wanted to make a call. And anyone on the party line could pick up their receiver and listen in to your conversation. I think single line service, which took until the early 1970s to become nearly universal, has allowed the telephone to fully develop into what we know it today, a way to make personal and business calls in a relaxed, comfortable manner. That we don't think about single line service as enabling the telephone is a good thing. You see, it's only when technology becomes secondary, when we no longer notice it, does it become truly liberating.

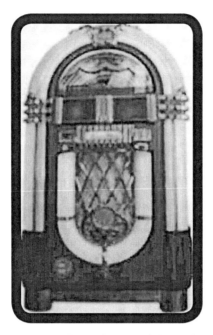

JUKEBOX FOR RECORDS

NOT A LOT OF ROOM FOR A LARGE FAMILY

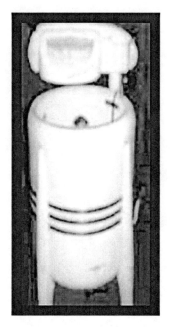

A "WRINGER TYPE" WASHING MACHINE

SMALL GAS STATIONS IN 1940s to 1950s.

This is my dear husband, Rol Lampe, that continues to enrich my life in love and joy and direction to God. He knew the way, we met, and our journey continued on together.

Ruth Kuehnl Lampe

Begin with God

CPSIA information can be obtained
at www.ICGtesting.com
Printed in the USA
FFOW04n1604200314
4381FF

9 781618 562388